Simple Pleasures

for the

Holidays

Simple Pleasures

for the

Holidays

A Treasury of Stories and Suggestions for Creating Meaningful Celebrations

Susannah Seton

CONARI PRESS
Berkeley, California

Conari Press books are distributed by Publishers Group West

Cover Photographs: Boy © Andre Gallant/Image Bank; Gifts © Steve Niedorf
    Photography/Image Bank; Candles © Kitarou Yokoi/Photonica
Cover Design: Ame Beanland
Book Design: Jennifer Brontsema
Interior Illustrations: Kathleen Edwards

For permission to excerpt from previously published material the author gratefully acknowledges: Excerpt from "Essential Holiday Ingredients" by Ann Michael from AOL's "Moms Online." Excerpt from *True Love: How to Make Your Relationship Sweeter, Deeper and More Passionate* by Daphne Rose Kingma; ©1991 by Daphne Rose Kingma; reprinted by permission of Conari Press. Excerpt from "Around the World with AOL: Celebrating the International Channel" [December 9, 1997]. Stories from various online bulletin boards forwarded to "Around the World with AOL." Excerpt from *Kwanzaa: An African-American Celebration of Cooking and Culture*; ©1991 by Eric V. Copage. Excerpts from *Simple Pleasures* by Robert Taylor, Susannah Seton, and David Greer; © 1996; reprinted by permission of Conari Press. "First Person: Holiday Memories" by Tanya Leno and Cherie Moreno first appeared in the *San Francisco Examiner*, December 21, 1997; reprinted by permission of the authors and the *San Francisco Examiner*. Excerpt from *Unplug the Christmas Machine* by Jo Robinson and Jean Coppock Staeheli; © 1982 by Jo Robinson and Jean Coppock Staeheli. Excerpts from "Grandma Jane's Home & Family Idea Exchange" at www.grandmanet.com. Excerpt from *Feeding the Body, Nourishing the Soul* by Deborah Kesten; © 1997 by Deborah Kesten; reprinted by permission of Conari Press.

Library of Congress Cataloging-in-Publication Data
     Seton, Susannah, 1952–
          Simple pleasures for the holidays : a treasury of stories and suggestions for creating
          meaningful celebrations / Susannah Seton.
               p.   cm.
          Includes index.
          ISBN 1–57324–135–0 (hardcover)
          ISBN 1–57324–515–1 (paperback)
               1. Holidays—United States—Miscellanea. I. Title
     GT4803.S48   1998
     394.26–dc21   98–20822
                                                                                                          CIP

Printed in the United States of America on recycled paper
     01 01 03   RRD (PB)   10 9 8 7 6 5 4 3 2

The aspects of things that are most important for us are hidden because of their simplicity and familiarity.

—Ludwig Wittgenstein

Contents

Acknowledgments ix

Conscious Celebration: The Simpler Way xi

Halloween 1

Mexican Day of the Dead 17

Guy Fawkes Day 29

Thanksgiving 35

Hanukkah 55

Winter Solstice 73

Christmas Eve 85

Christmas 95

Boxing Day 137

Kwanzaa 143

New Year's Eve 155

New Year's Day 169

Chinese New Year 179

'Id al-Fitr 189

Kids' and Adults' Birthdays 197

Index 231

Acknowledgments

Heartfelt thanks to all those who shared their special memories, recipes, and ideas for the holidays with me: Ame Beanland, Mindy Blechman, Shirley Bragg, Jennifer Brontsema, Celia Carrasco Berg, Christine Clouser, Heather Dever, Karen Edelman of Saul's Deli, Shelly Glennon, Will Glennon, Ida Greenberg, Husna Hakim, Roz Helfand, Allison Hoover O'Dell, Kay Howell, Esther Kirsch, Nina Lesowitz, Ana Li, Everton Lopez, Annette Madden, Katie Marceau, Laura Marceau, Donald McIlraith, Sandy Minella, Erin McCune, Meredith Morris, Barb Parmet, Lesa Porché, Patricia Renton, Gloria Ryan, Vincent Ryan, Lara Starr, Kendrick Van Gerpen, and Kristen Wurz.

A bouquet of thanks to my loving husband, Donald, who again typed much of this manuscript, and to my editor, Claudia Schaab of Conari Press, who kept me sane and picked up the pieces. Thanks also to the rest of the staff of Conari, who supported me in this and all my endeavors. It couldn't be a book without all of you: Jennifer, Suzanne, Laura, Robin, Sharon, Brenda, Nancy, Jay, Will, Nina, Everton, Tom, and Annette.

Special appreciation to Cathy DeForest, the Queen of Celebration, who shared with me an article she wrote entitled "The Art of Conscious Celebration" which I borrowed for the introduction. Her ideas helped inform my thinking. Also thanks to Margaret Wheatley, whose book, *A Simpler Way*, inspired the introduction's subtitle.

Conscious Celebration: The Simpler Way

We have two lives—
the ones we're given and the ones we make.

—Mary Chapin Carpenter

If you've picked up this book, chances are you are looking for ways to bring more meaning and less hype, more heart and less materialism, into the ways you celebrate the special days of your life. You are not alone; for the past few years retailers around the United States have bemoaned the fact that Americans are spending less and less during the Christmas holiday season, and the move to simplicity has been named by the Trends Research Institute as the social movement of the next ten years. We are coming to see that we have a choice as to how we will celebrate throughout the year.

The simplicity movement has a number of roots. One is environmental. Increasingly people are becoming aware that we are destroying the Earth with our overconsumption of natural resources, and are looking for ways to conserve those resources. Another is economic. Too many people have been forced into bankruptcy by spendthrift ways, or made to work insane hours to keep up an extravagant lifestyle. And most of us can't keep up even when we try—fully 70 percent of Americans earn about one-third less today, after inflation, than they did twenty years ago.

But the primary reason is that we are beginning to realize that the acquisition of material goods, the "keeping up with the Joneses," doesn't bring happiness, emotional fulfillment, or a sense of connection to nature, ourselves, and one another. "We have lost our souls," as writer Cathy DeForest described it, and we are longing for Spirit. The commercialization of all of our holidays has only served to exacerbate these feelings. No matter how much we get for our birthday, Christmas, or Hanukkah, we still feel empty. How often do we experience the holidays as drudgery—what to get Dad, he is so hard to shop for; another boring or painful meal with the relatives; too much work for the women as the men sit around; a fight with the wife because you forgot the card; a pinch in the wallet that will take months to recover from. . . .

The good news is that the holidays don't have to be expensive, meaningless, or filled with stress. Rather, they can be occasions to connect deeply with yourself, one another, and nature, to express creativity, to laugh, eat, and make merry together. Indeed, it is precisely these "extraordinary" times that give life much of its meaning. They give us a chance to experience what theologian Harvey Cox described as the interplay of our specialness with our commonness—everyone you know may be celebrating New Year's Eve, but only you and your family do it in *your* way. Indeed, the fact that you create your own personal rituals is precisely what makes a holiday special.

Writer Ann Michael gets to the heart of this: "For me, the spirit of Christmas is about letting the loving but messy little rituals become just as important as the solemn and graceful ones. It's about making room for everyone, especially children." While she is talking about Christmas, I think what she has to say goes to the heart of every holiday. When I asked people to write down their simple holiday pleasures, most people shared their family traditions. What makes them special and so enjoyable is the fact that they were done every year, but only on that particular occasion: making *Confetti Angel Food Cake* with pink peppermint boiled frosting for your daughter's birthday; polishing the silver menorah for Hannukah; getting the tree the day after Thanksgiving, or the day before Christmas; walking on the beach every Thanksgiving afternoon. It's not so much what you choose to do, but that you do it every year.

From the stories I received, I was reminded over and over that it's shared experiences, not objects, that we most value and remember. Very few people wrote about material goods—except those who received meaningful, heirloom objects such as a grandmother's engagement ring. What people remembered was the feelings that were created by being in certain circumstances: driving around every year with your sweetheart looking at the holiday lights, eating with all the relatives on Christmas Eve.

The more we use the holidays—the cycling of life through the wheel of time punctuated by special occasions—to create meaningful celebrations, the more we will feel satisfied, no matter our income. With this in mind, I offer *Simple Pleasures for the Holidays*. It's filled with stories by folks around the world to inspire you in your thinking about your own celebrations, as well as simple crafts, recipes, games, decorations, and gifts that you can make to enhance your enjoyment of the holidays. The idea is to choose a few meaningful items that you can make on your own to reduce the strain on your pocketbook and on the Earth, and to increase both the fun and the meaning of each celebration. When I was a kid, for example, I enjoyed making paper snowflakes for the windows much more than putting up any store-bought decoration. In using the book, don't neglect the index—my ordering of things is somewhat arbitrary. You might want to make the cake I have in the birthday section for Thanksgiving; the holiday napkin rings in Hanukkah for New Year's Eve; the bath powder in the Christmas section for Hanukkah.

You'll also find scattered throughout the book sections called "Easy Ideas for...." Most of these are suggestions for making a particular holiday more meaningful. These suggestions take nothing except your courage to risk asking the emotionally honest question, saying the heartfelt thing. I strongly encourage you to give at least one or two of them a try. I trust that you will discover that by taking the risk, you will create deep connections among those you are celebrating with.

Most likely you will find holidays here that you do not celebrate. I encourage you to read about each one and think about whether you would like to incorporate it somehow into your life. We celebrate for a variety of religious, social, cultural, and familial reasons. Creating conscious celebrations means thinking about each holiday and choosing to participate or not. Many folks these days are incorporating winter solstice celebrations into their lives out of a desire to honor their connection to nature. Over the past few years, many African Americans have begun to celebrate Kwanzaa, and many Caucasian families who have adopted daughters from China (myself included) are now celebrating Chinese New Year as a way of honoring their children's heritage.

Avoiding the Shoulds

To truly create conscious celebrations, as each holiday approaches, identify the essence of the holiday for you. What are the ingredients necessary for you and your family to enjoy it? What specific symbols, images, or words come to mind? It's important that you decide together what you want to do—remember, creating it should be as much fun as attending. While tradition is important, don't become a slave to it. Give yourself permission to say no (or yes). And don't let the "should's" ruin your fun. Just because you "always" did it before doesn't mean you always have to do it. Is it enjoyable for you to make three dozen latkes from scratch? If not, don't do it—or find a way to get lots of help. Perhaps it's time for someone else in the extended family to host the Thanksgiving bash; you've done it for the past twenty years.

For those who are blending traditions, whether because of marriage or remarriage, compromise is the order of the day. I have a friend whose kids go to their father's house on Christmas, so they always exchange presents with their mother on Epiphany; my friends Lara (Jewish) and John

(Christian) always celebrate both Hanukkah and Christmas. Again, the trick is to create more happiness, joy, and love, not chaos, division, or rancor. So think about what might work in your situation and be willing to be flexible while still creating some sense of tradition.

Easy Ideas for Pleasurable Holidays

- Remember—it's being together that counts. Not how beautiful your tree is, the perfection of your lemon meringue pie, or the spotlessness of the house (clean only the rooms guests will see).

- The more comfortable and relaxed everyone feels, the more the occasion will be happy. Don't try to do too much—too many activities, too much elaborate food will destroy the fun. And put away things you don't want little ones to ruin—why spend the whole day worrying that Matthew might spill cranberry juice on your white ottoman?

- If weather permits, consider meeting outside—at a park, a lake, or in the backyard. No cleaning required and no worries about breakage or spillage.

- Think quality, not quantity. A quiet holiday with four people you really care about will be much more pleasant than hosting a loud, noisy crowd of people who don't mean anything to you.

- Don't take family for granted. Be sure to express by your words and actions that you are happy to be together. My former in-laws used to bug my husband and me to attend all the holidays at the family home. But when we showed up, no one ever bothered to look up from the newspaper or the football game to greet us, everyone continued their solitary activities until it was time to eat. No wonder I didn't like going.

- No one decreed that every holiday required the hostess to make a full sit-down meal. Try potlucks, or cooking assignments (if you are a guest, bring your dish already prepared so you won't be taking up valuable oven or counter space), or getting together for coffee and desserts.

- It's OK to plan for what you want, but be willing to accept what actually happens. How many holidays have been ruined because the soufflé fell or the toddler refused to smile for the family photo? Remember, the feelings that you engender together are all that really matter!

Halloween

October 31

Listen! The wind is rising,
and the air is wild with leaves.
We have had our summer evenings,
now for October eves!

—Humbert Wolfe

On Her Own

My best Halloween memories come from the year when I was finally old enough to go out trick or treating unsupervised. It was the one night I could stay out late, roaming the neighborhood. I loved the sense of freedom. My friends and I would all meet at a particular house and we would go out together, giggling in the crisp night air. Having lived in the same neighborhood for years, we knew which houses had the best candy, which house had the man that gave out magic tricks, which houses were haunted. There even was one house where the people had made a maze out of cardboard boxes in their garage. It was completely dark except for light sticks sticking up every once in a while and you had to find your way out. Every so often a person would pop up out of nowhere and scare you. I was deliciously afraid.

Spirited Decorations

- Take inexpensive white tissue paper and cut it into free-form ghost and goblin shapes, then use double-stick tape to display them in your windows. Have ghoulish faces peeking in from corners or silly ones popping up over the edges. You can even put these on mirrors in your house.

- Make facial tissue ghosts. First wad up a piece of tissue or paper into a ball a little smaller than the size of a golf ball—this will serve as the ghost's head. Then put the ball in the center of another tissue and gently twist or gather the tissue around the head. White thread works well to secure the neck. Use a black felt-tip marker to draw a face—be careful, because the tissue will really soak up the ink, so err on the spare side when drawing. Then tie a piece of thread around the head and hang your ghost from the ceiling or doorway. It's really fun to do a whole bunch of these for party decorations or even do up a bunch of blank-faced ones and let your guests draw on the expressions.

- Place dry ice in a large container with a bit of water to simulate a witches' brew. Be sure to keep out of reach of kids; it burns!

- Hang a string of lights with orange and black bulbs.

3

Halloween

A Hearty Sendoff

My mother believed in fortifying us kids with a hot nourishing dinner before we set off for trick or treating. And she could not think of anything hardier than her famous Irish Lamb Stew. At the time, we thought it was a drag—we were too excited to eat, but she insisted that we have a bit before setting off. Now this is one of my favorite cold weather dinners—and I always have it on Halloween. My mother, who only married an Irishman and wasn't truly Irish herself, always made this with barley, not potatoes, but certainly potatoes are the traditional choice.

Lamb Stew

3 pounds boneless lamb
6 medium potatoes, sliced
3 large onions, sliced
3 large carrots, sliced
3 stalks celery, chopped
1 teaspoon thyme
1 teaspoon Tabasco sauce
1 bay leaf
Salt and pepper to taste
Water to cover

Arrange lamb, which should have a minimum of fat, in alternating layers with potatoes, onions, and carrots. Add the seasonings and just cover with water. Cover and either simmer on top of the stove or cook in a 325°F oven for 1½ to 2 hours or until meat is tender. Serves 6.

Stay at Home Fun

My mother didn't like us roaming the streets on Halloween—we didn't live in a very safe neighborhood—so she always created a traditional party for our friends and us instead: bobbing for apples, carving pumpkins and toasting the seeds (very delicious!), making and eating popcorn balls, peanut brittle, etc., and of course a haunted "house." It was always in the darkened basement; she would set up bowls of worms (cold spaghetti), fish eyes (Jell-O), and spider webs (cotton) for us to feel as we roamed from spot to spot. Scary music would be playing and someone would always jump out of the closet to scare us to death. We always had a great time, even as we got older and "jaded." In high school, we skipped the haunted house and played with the Ouija board and took turns levitating one another—it really worked, honest!

5

Halloween

Easy Ideas for Halloween Parties

- Hide your speakers outside and play a tape of scary noises.
- Serve roasted pumpkin seeds that kids can make after they

carve their jack-o-lanterns. Rinse well, toss with salt and vegetable oil and bake at 350° F for 30 minutes or until golden brown. Yummy.

- Make Ghoul-Aid. Make 1 package Grape Kool-Aid and 1 package Orange Kool-Aid according to directions. Combine and add 1 quart ginger ale. Stir and add ice.

- Try a Worm Dessert. Crumble enough Oreo cookies to make a crust and press into the bottom of a pie pan, reserving some for top. Fill with your favorite ice cream and sprinkle the remaining chocolate crumbs on top. Just before serving, add gummy worms.

- Have the kids come not in costume and have them paint one another's faces as a party activity. For four kids, mix 12 tablespoons cornstarch with 4 tablespoons flour. Stir in 1 cup water and 3 cups light corn syrup. Set aside ¼ of this mixture. Divide the rest into containers, adding 1 teaspoon (or more) food coloring for each color desired. With your fingers, apply the un-tinted mixture to each child's face, avoiding the eyes. (Older kids can do this for one another.) Allow to dry completely. Then use colored "paint" to add accents. Will wash right off with warm water and soap.

Old-Fashioned Delights

Here are four traditional Halloween treats that you can easily make for a party or for trick or treaters.

Caramel Corn

⅓ cup honey
¾ cup brown sugar
2 tablespoons butter or margarine
1 cup peanuts
3 quarts popped corn

Halloween

Preheat oven to 350°F. In a medium saucepan, heat the honey, brown sugar, and butter or margarine until melted.

On a large baking sheet, combine the peanuts and popcorn and spread in one layer. Pour the sugar mixture on top. Bake until crisp, about 10 to 15 minutes. Serves 4–6.

Aplets

2 cups applesauce
2 cups sugar
2 tablespoons unflavored gelatin
½ cup cold water
1½ cup chopped almonds
3 drops orange extract
powdered sugar

Butter an 8-inch baking pan. Cook applesauce and sugar in a medium saucepan until it gets very thick. While applesauce is cooking, sprinkle the gelatin into the water and let stand. Remove applesauce from heat, and stir in gelatin. Add almonds and orange extract and stir well. Pour into baking pan. Cover and let stand on the counter overnight; do not refrigerate. The next day, cut into squares and roll in powdered sugar. Will keep up to a week or so. Serves 12.

Classic Caramels

I tablespoon vegetable oil
¾ cup sugar
1½ cups heavy cream
I cup light corn syrup
3 tablespoons butter
2 teaspoons vanilla

Line an 8-inch square baking pan with foil, extending foil over edges of pan. Coat the foil with oil. In a large, heavy saucepan, combine the sugar, cream, and corn syrup. With a wooden spoon, stir continuously over medium heat until sugar is dissolved, about 5 minutes. To prevent crystallization, brush down the sides of the pot twice during the process with a pastry brush dipped in water.

Place a candy thermometer in the pot and cook, stirring, over medium-high heat until the temperature reaches 250° F, about half an hour. Remove from heat and add the butter and vanilla. Pour into foil-lined pan and let cool completely, at least 2 hours. Lift the caramel out of the pan with the edges of the foil. Coat a large knife with oil. Peel the foil off the caramel and cut the caramel into 8 equal strips with the oiled knife. Then cut each strip into 8 pieces. Wrap each caramel tightly in plastic wrap. Can be stored in a jar with a lid for up to 2 weeks. Makes 64.

Peanut Brittle

¼ cup water
I cup sugar
¼ teaspoon cream of tartar
½ cup light corn syrup
I½ cups roasted, unsalted peanuts
I tablespoon peanut butter
½ teaspoon salt
½ teaspoon baking soda

Halloween

Grease a large cookie sheet. In a large saucepan, bring the water to a boil and add the sugar and cream of tartar. Stir until sugar is dissolved. Stir in the corn syrup, place a candy thermometer in the pan, and cook over medium-high heat until temperature reaches 350°F. Remove from heat and stir in remaining ingredients. Pour onto prepared sheet. Let cool completely, then break into pieces. Can store in an airtight container for up to I week. Makes about I pound.

9

I'll Take the Trick

My favorite part of trick or treating was always the "trick" part. "Tee-peeing," or toilet-papering, yards was a favorite pastime of the kids in my small hometown, and Halloween provided the perfect opportunity to indulge in this naughty prank. My friends and I would ready for the evening with all the precision of a military strike. We'd borrow our brothers and father's hunting fatigues or dress in all-black sweatsuits, making sure our shirts were big enough to stuff at least six rolls of toilet paper up them. Most importantly, we'd start stockpiling the toilet paper weeks before as not to elicit suspicion. Our targets were usually people that we knew had papered our own yards in the past and sometimes even other friends—it was always done in sport. Half the time we'd get caught red-handed and wind up having to clean up the yards ourselves, but that didn't dampen the fun. The thrill of sneaking through the night, synchronizing our watches, staking out a pick-up point should we get separated, and shrieking when a victim's porch light came on—it was a heart-pounding adventure. I only pray that my yard-rolling feats are not visited back upon me now that I'm an adult. It's a big mess to clean up.

Mother Knows Best

My mother used to always make our Halloween costumes—
last year's holiday dress and some tinfoil made me a princess
with a diamond tiara, old overalls and some painted-on stub-
ble transformed me into a hobo, add some straw to the latter
and I was a scarecrow. One year I desperately wanted a store-
bought costume. You know the ones—a thin plastic smock
with a design printed on it and a plastic mask that you affix
to your head with a thread-thin piece of elastic. I wanted a
ghoulish one portraying a vampire with blood dripping from
his fangs and a black plastic cape that drooped from a smock
printed like a black suit with a gold medallion in the center of
the chest.

11

Halloween

After much wheedling, my mother conceded but warned
me that the mask would be uncomfortable and of the high
likelihood that my plastic garb wouldn't make it through the
night. I didn't care; I just wanted to be Count Dracula. After
a night of trick or treating where I encountered at least eight
other Count Draculas, sweated profusely under my plastic
cape (which ripped on a hedge at the second house I visited),
and struggled to see through the small eyeholes in my
scratchy mask, I realized how much better those homemade
costumes were. Sure, maybe there were other hobos or

princesses, but never one exactly like me. Maybe they carried a pack in a red bandanna but I had a beat-up satchel, or my crown had beads glued on it where others didn't. The next year I was the Hunchback of Notre Dame with my father's flannel shirt and a towel stuffed on my shoulder. I had a wonderful time galumphing around with my friends—a gypsy, a queen, a policeman, and a miserable kid in a plastic Spiderman get-up from the five-and-dime.

Easy Ideas for Simple Costumes

- *Bumble Bee:* Take a very large yellow sweater vest or buy an inexpensive yellow sweatshirt and cut off the sleeves. Make stripes with wide, black electrical tape all around your vest. Wear a black turtleneck underneath and black leggings or sweatpants. Make antennas out of black pipe cleaners and pom-pom balls and affix them to a headband. Cut wings out of white tulle or netting and gather and pin them onto your back. If you want a stinger, fashion one out of pipe cleaners.

- *Vampire Victim:* Wear a pair of pajamas or a nightgown (wear a bodysuit or thermals underneath if you need to). Powder your face or use make-up to make your face and neck very pale. Use black or purple make-up to make dark circles under your eyes. Finish by making two puncture marks on your neck and some ghoulish blood drips with red make-up. If you want, you can wear fangs and be a newly created vampire.

- *El Niño:* Wear heavy duty raingear: a slicker and a rain hat with rubber boots and carry an umbrella

- *Mummy:* The best Halloween costume I ever had was one my father and I improvised when I was about ten. I wanted to be a mummy and he wrapped me up in surgical gauze, one limb at a time, then my torso, then my neck and face, leaving slits for the eyes. I came unwrapped before the night was through, but that only added to the fun!

13

Halloween

Giving Back

When I was in junior high school, I used to go around the neighborhood collecting money for UNICEF on Halloween. Does anyone still do that? It was great—an excuse to dress in costume, and be out late at night even though I was too "old" for trick or treating. I really loved collecting money for poor kids around the world—and had the added bonus of receiving candy at almost every stop!

A Family Affair

My grandmother had a unique Halloween tradition. Rather than letting us go out trick or treating, she would create a basket with a beautiful ribbon for each of us cousins and hide the whole basket. Then she would give us a piece of the ribbon—a different color for each child—and tell us to find the basket with that colored ribbon. We were carefully instructed not to tell anyone if we found other baskets, so we would always try to be as sneaky as possible. (Not always successfully, I might add.) As we got older, she got more and more clever about the hiding places. She then progressed to having us hunt just for the ribbons—much more difficult to find than a whole basket; when we returned with our ribbon, we would be rewarded with our basket. Then she hid only tiny pieces of ribbon. We all loved it because she always made it hard, but not impossible. (The last time we did it, however, as young adults, some of us looked for hours and finally she had to give us hints. The following year, the five cousins turned tables and made her hunt!) We would then all get to eat as much candy as we wanted and then have a sleep over in the living room at Grandma's house—complete with scary stories and the appearance of a ghost (Grandpa).

Never Too Old

My husband and I were in the process of adopting a baby and it was seeming to take forever. I was feeling sorry for myself and despairing of ever having a child to create special occasions for, when Halloween rolled around again. To pull me out of my funk, Don took me down to the local pumpkin patch and made me pick out three pumpkins—one for each of us and our baby to be. We came home and carved them—I hadn't done that in years—and I enjoyed it so much that I was pulled right out of my funk.

15

Halloween

Mexican Day of the Dead

November 2

He who fears death cannot enjoy life.

—Spanish proverb

Honoring the Dead

El Dia de los Muertos is celebrated in Mexico and in Mexican American communities on November 2 as the day when the souls of the dead return. The living do everything in their power to make this day one of pleasure and delight for their guests. They cook the favorite foods of their departed relatives and friends, and decorate their houses with candles and flowers to guide their guests to the right homes. Long before sunrise, people stream to the cemeteries to welcome the dead souls with flowers, candles, and food that is often shaped in the symbols of death: chocolate hearses, sugar funeral wreaths, candy skulls and coffins. In many homes, the Indians set up *ofrendas,* or altars to the departed. These are decked with lighted candles, special foods, and whatever the dead enjoyed when they were alive.

Comforting the Living

My six-year-old son's father died and Michael was having a hard time adjusting. I decided to celebrate the Day of the Dead with him (he is Mexican American on his father's side). We built an altar for his father, Damian, in Michael's room.

On top, Michael put a drawing he made of his father and him, Damian's favorite hat, and his favorite food. Early in the morning when it was still dark, we went to the cemetery and placed candles, flowers, and food on Damian's grave, and had a picnic breakfast. All around us, people were eating and talking, candles blazing. Michael felt much better after that— the idea that his father comes once a year to see him was greatly comforting.

19

Mexican Day of the Dead

Viva la Vida!

Dia de los Muertos, or Day or the Dead, has great meaning for me. My mother died when I was eight, so I grew up with the knowledge that life is transient and death is near us always. It is not a morbid feeling, but more a realization of the importance of really living life. The Mexicans celebrate this day with a combination of respect, solemnity, and great humor.

For the last four years, I have had a party on that day. Friends and I build a large, colorful altar, and everyone brings photos and mementos of departed souls to place on the altar. Over the years, a ceremony has evolved. I burn copal, the incense that is said to guide the deceased to the altar. Then, those who wish stand in front of the altar and show the photo they brought and tell stories about that person. It is a power-ful experience, with lots of tears and laughter. The evening is a remarkable combination of eating great Mexican food, drinking, having fun, and opening ourselves to our memo-ries. By remembering those who were here before us, we know ourselves better. In our society there is no place for an event like this. It is a celebration of life and who we are.

20

Glorious Food

No Day of the Dead celebration is complete without a won-derful meal. Here's a Mexican-inspired dinner that is easy to prepare.

Tomato Avocado Salad

1 small jalapeño, minced
¼ cup freshly squeezed lime juice
½ cup extra-virgin olive oil
⅛ teaspoon salt, plus salt to taste
1 clove garlic, minced
1 3/4 pounds ripe tomatoes, cut into large chunks
1 sweet onion, sliced ¼ inch thick and separated into rings
2 ripe avocados, peeled, pitted, and cut into slices
pepper to taste

In a small glass bowl, whisk together jalapeño, lime juice, oil, ⅛ teaspoon salt, and garlic. In a large serving bowl, place the tomatoes and onion, then toss with vinaigrette until well coated. Add the avocados and salt and pepper to taste, and toss. Serves 4.

Tamale Pie

1½ cups cold water
1½ cups corn meal
1½ teaspoons salt
2 cups water
1 pound ground beef
½ cup chopped onion
2 tablespoons flour
1 teaspoon chili powder
1 pound can chopped tomatoes
1 8-ounce can tomato sauce
1 cup whole kernel corn, drained

21

*Mexican Day
of the Dead*

Grease a 2-quart casserole. Preheat oven to 350°F. Combine cold water and corn meal until well blended. In a medium saucepan, bring water and ½ teaspoon salt to a boil. Add corn meal mixture, stirring constantly, bring to a boil. Partially cover pan; cook slowly 7 minutes on low heat, stirring often. When cooked, place cornmeal in the casserole, covering the bottom and sides.

Cook beef and onion in a frying pan until beef is brown and crumbly. Stir in flour, remaining 1 teaspoon salt, and chili powder.

Add tomatoes, breaking them up into chunks with spoon. Stir in tomato sauce and corn. Spoon into cornmeal-lined casserole. Bake in oven until hot and bubbly, 40 to 45 minutes. Makes 6 servings.

Homemade Flour Tortillas

4 cups flour
1¼ teaspoon salt
6 tablespoons vegetable shortening
approximately 1¼ cups boiling water

Sift together the flour and salt into a large bowl. Mix the shortening in by hand, until the mixture resembles cornmeal and feels slightly gritty to the touch. Stir in enough boiling water that the dough sticks together. Place the dough on a floured surface and knead for approximately 5 minutes. Form dough into a ball, place inside the bowl, and cover with plastic wrap. After approximately 30 minutes, divide the dough into 10 to 12 balls, and roll each flat with a well-floured rolling pin. Cook in a cast-iron skillet over medium heat, about 20 seconds on each side. Makes 10 to 12 tortillas.

Mexican Wedding Cookies

While these traditionally are "wedding cookies," they are often served at other festive occasions as well.

½ cup powdered sugar
1 cup butter, softened
1 teaspoon vanilla
2¼ cups flour
¼ teaspoon salt
¾ cup chopped nuts, optional
additional powdered sugar

Cream together the ½ cup sugar, butter, and vanilla in a large bowl. Sift in the flour and salt. Add the nuts, if using. Cover and chill the dough for 2 hours in the refrigerator or 10 minutes in the freezer.

Preheat oven to 400°F. Roll the dough into 1-inch balls and place on an ungreased cookie sheet. Bake until set, about 10 minutes. While still warm, roll the cookies in powdered sugar. Makes 4 dozen.

23

*Mexican Day
of the Dead*

Mexican Hot Chocolate

This is fabulous, the perfect thing for a cold fall evening. If you have cinnamon-flavored Ibarra chocolate, use it instead of the semisweet and omit the cinnamon and brown sugar.

4 cups milk
3 3-inch long cinnamon sticks, broken in half
30 whole cloves
I teaspoon aniseed
5 ounces semisweet chocolate, chopped
2 tablespoons unsweetened cocoa powder
2 tablespoons brown sugar

In a large, heavy saucepan over medium heat, bring the milk, cinnamon, cloves, and aniseed to a simmer. Add the remaining ingredients and whisk until the chocolate melts. Remove from heat, cover and let steep for 45 minutes. Serves 4.

Celebrating Life

A friend of mine has invited me to a *Dia de los Muertos* party for the past two years in a row. I was intrigued by the concept but a little leery—fearing it to be a morbid or unholy endeavor. Like many people, I was taught that death is a very reverent subject to be spoken of in hushed tones and described in euphemistic terms like "passing on" and "gone to a better place." To purposefully initiate contact with the dead was dangerous and sacrilegious. Last year, though, my curiosity—aided by the reassurance of my friend—got the better of me and I attended with her. I was instructed to bring a photo or favorite object of a dead loved one(s). I gathered up three pictures: my father, my brother, and my aunt, said a prayer for forgiveness, and left with my husband for the party.

Even though I had read about the gaiety of these gatherings I still expected it to be somewhat somber. Imagine my surprise when the door opened to reveal a room awash with people laughing and talking, music boldly playing, and an ebullient spirit filling the entire house. All this surrounding a beautiful altar glowing with candles, draped in exuberant colors, sparked with flowers, and crowned with colorful paper banners. Woven throughout were photos and personal effects: shoes, hats, a sewing box, pieces of jewelry placed carefully here and there, and people all around, admiring the objects and talking about the people they represented. It was breathtaking in its tribute. My pessimism and fear vanished and I saw this tradition for what it is—a hope-filled celebration and a wonderful opportunity to remember and honor the dead. After a fabulous dinner, people were invited to share stories and memories of their loved ones. Some were touching and poignant while others were hysterical and irreverent. I didn't feel compelled to participate, but sat there with a distinct feeling that my father, brother, and aunt were with me and honored. It was an event that truly blessed me.

25

Mexican Day of the Dead

I'm very grateful for the experience and hope to participate again in this wonderful holiday.

Homemade Candles

Candles are an important part of the *Dia de Los Muertos* holiday. And if you want to make your own candles, catalogs such as Hearthsong (800-432-6314) have candle-making kits. Or you can try the old standard we used to make in grade school. It's easy, but be careful—paraffin must be heated over low heat or it can explode. Never put it directly on the stove—only over a water bath

> block of paraffin (to equal 1 quart)
> crayon bits for coloring
> 1 half gallon coffee can
> 1 wick
> 1 pencil or chopstick
> 1 quart waxed cardboard milk or juice container,
> washed and top cut off

Put the paraffin and crayon bits in the coffee can and place the can in a pan of water on the stove to create a double boiler. Melt the paraffin over low heat. Be sure to keep it over a very low flame because paraffin explodes easily when overheated.

While wax is melting, tie wick onto pencil or chopstick and place in the cardboard so that the pencil keeps the wick upright When wax is melted, pour carefully into the milk or juice container and allow to harden completely overnight. Cut away container. Makes one pillar candle.

*Mexican Day
of the Dead*

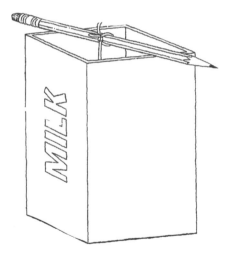

Guy Fawkes Day

November 5

Please to remember
The Fifth of November
Gunpowder, treason, and plot;
I know no reason
Why Gunpowder Treason
Should ever be forgot.

—Mother Goose

Neighborhood Revelry

November in England is an oppressive month. The sullen, leaden overhang of clouds ensures dank and dour days. By late afternoon, fog and darkness creep in to enclose the damp nights. Only the promised glow of Guy Fawkes Day on the fifth entices us from our hearth fires. Also known as Bonfire Night, its roots, like most English festivals, are buried in the past. In the early 1600s, a disgruntled Guy Fawkes had planned to blow up the Houses of Parliament by placing barrels of gunpowder in their cellars. The plot was discovered and the misguided Guy and his fellow conspirators were arrested and executed. The event is still celebrated. (And in the tradition-bound, boneheaded British way, the cellars of the Houses of Parliament are still searched prior to each new session.)

In the days leading up to the bonfire, cheeky small boys with soot-darkened faces prowl the streets, dragging on go-carts effigies of Mr. Fawkes fashioned from old clothes stuffed with straw. They knock on doors demanding, "Penny for the Guy," to buy their fireworks. Our neighborhood, like many others, goes to work to build its bonfire on a nearby empty lot. It's a community effort. Anything burnable, including old furniture, is hauled along to the fire. By the fifth, the bonfire is a handsome structure, standing some fifteen feet high. Local kids guard against marauding, wood-stealing rival groups.

On the evening of Guy Fawkes Day, the excitement gathers around the preparing of flasks of hot soup and cocoa and the assembling of fireworks. Finally, bundled up to the eyeballs against the dripping darkness, we join the stream of neighbors heading to the party.

With great ceremony the fire is lit. We "ooh" and "aah" as we watch the flames climb skyward. When the fire has truly caught, the Guy effigies are tossed into it with much booing, laughter, and applause. Fireworks are set off. Flushed young faces, eyes-a-glitter, gaze with awe. The fire crackles, shooting sparks in all directions. Breath drifts upward to the stars poking through the cloud cover. Rockets explode, cascading streams of shimmering light. Freezing hands clutch ignored hot drinks. The night is magical, wondrous. A brief brilliance against the desolate dark. For a moment, bleak November is vanquished. This, perhaps, is our real reason for holding on to this archaic ritual.

31

Guy Fawkes Day

Onion Soup

Whether or not you celebrate Guy Fawkes Day, it does get cold around this time of year. What better way to get warm than with a wonderfully rich Onion Soup—truly a simple pleasure?

I pound large white onions
½ cup unsalted butter
I cup dry white wine
7 cups beef stock
3 fresh thyme sprigs or ¼ teaspoon dried thyme
Salt and freshly ground pepper
½ day-old baguette loaf
2 cups shredded Swiss or Gruyere cheese

Cut the onions in half through the stem end, then again crosswise into thin slices. In a large saucepan over medium heat, melt the butter. Add the onions and wine and sauté, stirring frequently over medium heat, until onions are very soft and liquid is evaporated, about 15 minutes.

Pour in the stock, add the thyme, salt and pepper to taste, and bring to a boil. Reduce heat to medium and simmer, stirring often until flavors are combined, about 15 minutes.

Preheat the broiler. Cut the baguette into 6 slices. Ladle soup into 6 ovenproof bowls and place them on a wire rack or baking sheet. Place a bread slice on top of each bowl and top the slice with a liberal sprinkling of cheese. Broil 3 to 5 minutes, until cheese is melted and bubbly. Serve immediately. Serves 6.

Pumpkin Bread

Here's a wonderful fall bread that will be a tasty accompaniment to the soup.

33

Guy Fawkes Day

3 cups sugar
1 cup salad oil
4 eggs, beaten
1 16-ounce can pumpkin
3½ cups sifted flour
2 teaspoons baking soda
2 teaspoons salt
1 teaspoon baking powder
1 teaspoon nutmeg
1 teaspoon allspice
1 teaspoon cinnamon
½ teaspoon ground cloves
⅔ cup water

Generously grease and flour two 9-by-5 inch loaf pans. Preheat oven to 350°F. Cream sugar and oil in a large bowl. Add eggs and pumpkin; mix well. Sift together flour, baking soda, salt, baking powder, nutmeg, allspice, cinnamon, and cloves. Add to pumpkin mixture alternately with water. Mix well after each addition.

Pour into two loaf pans. Bake for 1½ hours, until loaves test done. Let stand for 10 minutes. Remove from pans to cool. Makes two loaves.

Thanksgiving

November 25

Let us, on the day set aside for this purpose,
give thanks to the Ruler of the universe for the
strength which He has vouchsafed us to carry on our
daily labors and the hope that lives within us
of the coming of a day when peace and the productive
activities of peace shall reign on every continent.

—Franklin D. Roosevelt,
Thanksgiving Day proclamation, October 31, 1939

Walking to Dinner

For me, the key to a pleasurable Thanksgiving is not the food, but the annual afternoon hike before the meal. Some years, we walk on the beach; others, we hike in the mountains. No matter where we walk, we always take along a picnic basket filled with appetizers and drinks. Timing is critical since we like to include the setting sun in our vistas while not getting caught in the dark on the way back to the turkey. It is in the spirit of thankfulness that we make the excursions so that when we sit down at the table, we are truly thankful to be eating with friends.

Give Me Stuffing

For me, Thanksgiving is just an excuse to eat stuffing. In fact, I think of turkey as merely the container for my mother's traditional oyster dressing. And it has to be consumed only at Thanksgiving—somehow the rest of the year it just doesn't taste right. I pile it high on my plate, garnish it with a few pickles and a dollop of cranberry sauce, and I'm in heaven.

Dried Fruit Stuffing

Stuffing is definitely a Thanksgiving tradition and every person has a preference—cooked inside the turkey or not, with the giblets or not—as to what ingredients to include. The following recipe, adapted from the Tomato Fresh Food Cafe in Vancouver, is not exactly traditional. But it is delicious.

1 pound Italian sausage, casing removed
½ pound bacon, cut into ½-inch pieces
¼ cup butter
3 large leeks, sliced (white and light green parts only)
1 large onion, diced
2 carrots, diced
3 large stalks celery with leaves, diced
2 cups dried prunes, chopped
1 cup dried apricots, chopped
2 tablespoons dried thyme
14 ounces brown bread, cut into ½-inch cubes
and baked at 350°F for 15 minutes
1⅓ cup turkey or chicken broth
3 eggs, beaten

37

Thanksgiving

In a large frying pan, cook the sausage and bacon until slightly golden, stirring frequently. Remove with a slotted spoon. Drain the remaining fat and add butter to the pan. Sauté the leeks, onions, carrots, and celery until soft. Remove from heat, stir in the dried fruit and thyme. Add the bread cubes, broth, eggs, sausage, and bacon, and stir well. Turn into a large baking dish, cover, and bake at

350°F for 45 minutes. Remove cover and bake for another 15 minutes. Makes 14 servings.

Visiting Grandma

We lived in Massachusetts growing up, and Grandma lived in Maine. So we didn't see her a lot. But every Thanksgiving vacation, we would pile into the car and make the drive to her house. We three kids always looked forward to it because Grandma was full of fun. She would always greet us with a big "Allo darlings" in her heavy French accent and we would play cards and laugh. But the best part for me was Grandma's homemade fudge. I could never get enough of that creamy (no nuts for me!), rich taste. Those visits were a long time ago now, but Thanksgiving still means fudge to me.

Ten-Minute Fudge

3 squares (1 ounce each) unsweetened chocolate
4 tablespoons butter
4½ cups sifted powdered sugar
⅓ cup instant nonfat dry milk
½ cup light or dark corn syrup

1 tablespoon water
1 teaspoon vanilla
½ cup chopped nuts, optional

Grease an 8-inch square pan. Melt chocolate and butter in the top of a 2-quart double boiler over hot water. Meanwhile, sift together sugar and dry milk in a medium bowl.

Stir corn syrup, water, and vanilla extract into chocolate-butter mixture. Stir in sifted sugar and dry milk in two additions. Continue stirring until mixture is well blended and smooth.

Remove from heat. Stir in nuts if using. Pour into pan. Cool. Cut into squares. Makes 24 2-inch squares.

39

Thanksgiving

The Pleasure of Gratitude

At the end of almost every family meal, and certainly at each Thanksgiving, my grandfather would lean back in his chair, and proudly say to my grandmother and all the rest of us at the table, "Naomi, that was the best meal I ever had." It got to be something of a family joke, but the truth was, it was obvious he meant it every time.

Favorite Foods

Thanksgiving is the time when families get very particular about their traditional foods. The following are two of the standards of the American table. If by chance you have somehow missed one or the other, you owe it to yourself to at least give them a try.

Candied Sweet Potatoes

I cup dark corn syrup
½ cup firmly packed dark brown sugar
2 tablespoons corn oil margarine
12 medium sweet potatoes, cooked,
peeled, and halved lengthwise
handful miniature marshmallows, optional

Preheat oven to 350°F. In a small saucepan, heat corn syrup, brown sugar, and margarine to boiling; reduce heat and simmer 5 minutes. Pour ½ cup of the syrup into a 13-by-9-by-2-inch baking dish. Arrange potatoes, overlapping if necessary, in syrup. Top with remaining syrup. Add marshmallows if using. Bake, basting often, for 20 minutes, until well glazed. Makes 12 servings.

Cranberry Apple Waldorf

3 envelopes unflavored gelatin
⅓ cup sugar
1 cup boiling water
3½ cups cranberry juice cocktail
1 cup chopped apple
½ cup chopped celery
⅓ cup chopped walnuts

41

Thanksgiving

In a large bowl, mix gelatin and sugar; add boiling water and stir until gelatin is completely dissolved. Add cranberry juice; chill until mixture has the consistency of unbeaten egg whites. Fold in apple, celery, and walnuts; pour into 8- or 9-inch square pan and chill until firm. To serve, cut into squares. Makes about 8 servings.

Thanksgiving Centerpiece

Here's an idea that is so simple you won't believe how good it will look. This Thanksgiving, why not decorate your table-top with a collection of gourds and squashes. In the center of your arrangement, place the "Mayflower." To make, find a large gourd in the shape of a boat and decorate with skewer masts and paper cutout sails. Finish off by scattering fall leaves, pine cones, and acorns among the squashes.

Love of Mincemeat

Twenty-five years ago, when I was in college, I fell in love with a wonderful man and decided to make him a batch of mincemeat cookies on his birthday in late November. Now, normally I am no baker, and cookies in particular drive me crazy because they take so long—you can't just mix them up and throw them in the oven. Each batch must be carefully watched to avoid burning and the whole process seems interminable. However, this was love, so I dragged out my mother's recipe, which she made each year for Thanksgiving, and gave it the old college try. Well, he loved them—and so did everyone else who tried them.

They became a tradition for me to make at Thanksgiving—one batch for him, and one for wherever I was going for Thanksgiving dinner. And although my love relationship with the man ended a long time ago, we have remained good friends and each year he receives his cookies on November 25, no matter where he is. (Since he's been living on the east coast and I on the west coast for the past seven years, they have become the most expensive cookies in the world when Federal Express charges are added in.) In general, I still hate making cookies, but the pleasure I get from pleasing him and the comfort I feel from the continuity of the tradition makes the effort totally worthwhile.

Mincemeat Cookies

Even if you swear you hate mincemeat, give these a try—
they are very tasty and quite unique. I've never met a person
who didn't love them.

1 cup shortening
1½ cups sugar
3 eggs
3 cups unsifted flour
1 teaspoon baking soda
½ teaspoon salt
1½ cups ready-to-use mincemeat (in the jar,
not the box; if you buy the boxed kind,
follow the recipe on the box because
it is drier and proportions are different)

43

Thanksgiving

Preheat oven to 375°F and grease a baking sheet. In a large bowl,
beat shortening and sugar until fluffy. Add the eggs and mix well.
Gradually add in the dry ingredients, mixing well after each addition. Stir in mincemeat and combine well. Drop the mixture by
rounded teaspoonfuls, 2 inches apart, onto baking sheet. Bake 8 to
10 minutes or until lightly browned. For crispy cookies, allow to
cool completely before covering; for softer cookies, cover when just
slightly cooled. Makes about 6 dozen.

Pepper-Coated Lamb

We always serve this delicious lamb at Thanksgiving because no one in our family likes turkey. I always make it with roasted potatoes that I baste with the same marinade. We've never had a guest who didn't love it. We adapted it years ago from *The Silver Palate Cookbook*. It is spicy, so be forewarned!

I tablespoon each whole green, white
(or pink), and black peppercorns
I teaspoon dried rosemary
6 cloves garlic, crushed
½ cup each raspberry vinegar and red wine
¼ cup soy sauce
I boneless leg of lamb, about 5 pounds
2 tablespoons Dijon mustard

With a mortar and pestle, crush the peppercorns together. Combine I tablespoon of this mixture (reserve the rest) with the rosemary, garlic, vinegar, wine, and soy sauce in a glass dish large enough to hold the lamb when untied. Place lamb flat in marinade and marinate overnight (two days is even better!), turning occasionally.

Preheat oven to 350°F. Remove lamb and set marinade aside. Roll up the lamb and tie with kitchen string. Spread mustard all over the lamb and then pat reserved peppercorns onto the meat, coating it completely. Place in a roasting pan and pour marinade in the bottom of the pan.

Roast until done, about 18 minutes per pound. Serve with marinade. Serves 8.

A Chinese Thanksgiving

Thanksgiving has always been something of a cursed day in the annals of my family's history. Perhaps it began with the year, shortly after my parents were married, when my mother had prepared a banquet for her new and definitely disapproving in-laws, and treated them to an unexpected shower of smelly sludge when the disposal backed up. Or the year that the fresh-from-the-oven turkey did a freestyle wobble roll across the white dining room carpet. Most vivid in my mind is the arrival of two fire trucks and an ambulance when a neighbor saw a veritable pillar of smoke rising from our kitchen window, resulting from my aunt's overcooked cherry pie. At any rate, before I was much into elementary school, our Thanksgiving dinners were served in style at a variety of local restaurants, primarily Chinese. Living in a year-round resort community, we never lacked for a venue for our celebration, and always exulted in the thought of a clean, empty, leftover-free kitchen. Now that our extended family has grown, we have gradually, and sometimes grudgingly,

45

Thanksgiving

returned to the traditional feast. Call me old-fashioned, but while I truly enjoy participating in this all-American tradition, the last Thursday of November just isn't the same for me without moo goo gai pan and green tea!

Easy Ideas for Creating Connection

- Say thanks. If you have trouble knowing what to say, you might want to pick up a copy of *A Grateful Heart: Daily Blessings for the Evening Meal from Buddha to The Beatles* by M. J. Ryan. Or hold hands and go around in a circle, saying one after another: "May the love that is in my heart pass from my hand to yours."

- Go around the table, each person naming one thing they are particularly grateful for this year.

- Ask each person to speak of who or what has been the greatest teacher in their life and why.

- Tell a story of how you celebrated Thanksgiving when you were a child.

- Invite the new person at the office who just relocated, or someone you know will be alone, to your home for Thanksgiving dinner and include him or her in your traditions.

Cranberry Delight

My favorite part of Thanksgiving is the cranberry sauce. It's the uniqueness of it that I love, I think, because I never have it any other time during the year. I might enjoy preparing it even more than eating it. No canned cranberry jelly for me. Beginning in high school, I was the official sauce-maker in my household; following in my mother's footsteps, I used the trusty basic recipe on the bag of cranberries. I loved how in just a few minutes, the berries would pop and what was one minute a bunch of discreet berries would suddenly become one entity. I never failed to enjoy the alchemical magic.

47

Thanksgiving

In my thirties, I began to branch out, to experiment with all kinds of variations on the theme. I never liked the recipes with orange peel. For years, I produced a very sophisticated sauce that contained boiled onions, thyme, and butter that I, but apparently no one else, loved. But now I have finally perfected what I consider to be the ultimate cranberry relish. Everywhere I go for Thanksgiving I get asked for the recipe. Don't be scared off by the ingredients!

Spicy Cranberry Relish

1 tablespoon vegetable oil
½ medium onion, diced
1 jalapeño pepper, diced
1 heaping tablespoon grated ginger
1 garlic clove, minced
⅓ cup cider vinegar
½ cup dry red wine
1 cup brown sugar
1 teaspoon ground pepper
1 teaspoon cinnamon
½ teaspoon ground allspice
½ teaspoon ground coriander
½ teaspoon ground cloves
¼ teaspoon ground nutmeg
2 sprigs thyme
1 small bay leaf
3 cups cranberries, washed and picked over
2 pears, peeled and diced
½ cup raisins

In a large saucepan, heat the oil over medium heat. Add the onion, jalapeño pepper, ginger, and garlic and sauté, stirring often, until onion is translucent. Add vinegar, wine, brown sugar, herbs, and spices. Simmer, stirring often, until syrupy, about 20 minutes.

Stir in cranberries, pears, and raisins. Simmer until cranberries pop, about 10–15 minutes. Remove the bay leaf and serve at room temperature. Makes 4 cups.

On the Beach

My favorite Thanksgiving was also the occasion of one of the worst thunderstorms in Hawaii's history. We had all gone to a friend's beach house for the weekend, only to find ourselves literally imprisoned in the house nearly all of Thanksgiving day by the record-breaking waves and lashing rain that rocked the tiny cottage. The storm finally broke just as we were finishing dinner, and the children were the first out the door and onto the deserted, storm-tossed beach. The world seemed to have been washed completely clean, but the waves had littered the beach with the most astounding panoply of treasures—shells and starfish, buoys, bottles, and other fascinating flotsam. I was the undisputed object of envy when I came upon a fist-sized, completely clear glass ball, bobbing tranquilly in the shore break. A passing beachcomber informed us that it was a Japanese fishing buoy, broken loose many thousands of miles away, that had gradually made its way to this small bay. What a magical treasure this tiny, fragile object was—I have long since forgotten what became of that small glass buoy, but I will never forget the awe and respect it inspired in me for the endless ocean and the rolling tide.

49

Thanksgiving

Broccoli Salad

I don't know about anyone else, but with all the rich food at Thanksgiving, I always long for something simple and green as a complement. Here's a vegetable recipe that goes well with just about anything—and it's good for you too.

1 bunch broccoli, cut into bite-sized pieces
1 garlic clove, pressed
3 tablespoons balsamic vinegar
6 tablespoons olive oil
salt and pepper to taste
5 ounces roasted red peppers (⅓ of a 15-ounce jar)
½ cup feta cheese, crumbled

Steam the broccoli until tender, about 7 minutes. Run under cold water and place on a large platter. In a small bowl, combine the garlic, vinegar, oil, salt, and pepper. Pour over broccoli and toss to coat. Sprinkle the peppers and cheese on top. Serves 4.

Easy Ideas for Thanksgiving Decorations

- Roll up your fabric napkins and tie with brown twine. Place a cinnamon stick or a leaf under the twine. Make a knot one inch from the end of the twine, and unravel the twine up to the knot.

- Use fall leaves as place cards. First dip in warm soapy water, rinse, and allow to air-dry. Press between the leaves of a heavy book and allow to dry for at least a week. When you remove leaves, handle carefully because leaves can tear easily. Using a gold marker, carefully write the name of each person on a leaf and place on table.

- Create a bed of leaves at each place for a placemat. Wash the leaves as described above the day before and arrange artfully on the table.

- Decorate yourselves with paper collars and Pilgrim hats; kids love it!

51

Thanksgiving

Giving Yourself

My husband and I are retired and live in Cape Cod, far away from the rest of our family. We used to feel sorry for ourselves at holidays such as Thanksgiving—no one to cook the traditional big meal for. Then we hit on volunteering at the local homeless shelter. We cook a full meal with all the trimmings—keeping some for ourselves—and then head for the shelter for the noon meal. We add our food to the mix and help serve. Later we come home and eat ourselves. It's a wonderful way to help out—and help ourselves feel better at the same time.

Cranberry Punch

This festive warm drink is nonalcoholic, so it can be enjoyed by everyone at the Thanksgiving table.

6 cups cranberry juice
2 cups lemonade
½ teaspoon each ground cinnamon,
cloves, and allspice
1 cup sugar
2 lemons, thickly sliced
24 whole cloves

Simmer all ingredients, except lemons and whole cloves, for 15 minutes. While the punch is cooking, stud the lemons with the cloves. When punch is ready, place in punchbowl or crockpot and float the lemons on top. Serves 12.

A Neighborhood Thanksgiving

The best Thanksgiving I ever spent was one where I was invited to a neighborhood celebration in Charlotte, South Carolina. Apparently, the people who live in the Sharon Hills Road area have been getting together for a barbeque for over fifty years. I had just moved to town and was far away from my family. I met one of the families who lived in the neighborhood and they suggested I come along. It was a day-long event filled with food (the oysters were my favorite), games, and a friendly atmosphere. Everyone pitched in to help; even me—I was on the cleanup detail. I met a lot of great folks, and it sure beat sitting alone in my room eating dried-out turkey!

Thanksgiving

Persimmon Pudding

This is a variation on a traditional Thanksgiving dessert. Persimmons are in season around Thanksgiving. They also make lovely centerpieces, either on the branch in a vase or clustered together with pomegranates.

3 large, very ripe persimmons
4 eggs
½ cup brown sugar
6 tablespoons canola oil
2 teaspoons vanilla extract
2 cups flour
I teaspoon baking soda
½ teaspoon salt
2 teaspoons ground cinnamon
½ teaspoon nutmeg
I teaspoon ground ginger

Grease a pudding mold or small baking dish (it must be able to fit into a large pot). Peel and mash the persimmons, removing any seeds (there should be about 2 cups of mash). In a large bowl, beat the eggs, then add the oil, sugar, and vanilla and beat until eggs are fluffy. Add the persimmons. Sift the flour, baking soda, salt, cinnamon, nutmeg, and ginger in a separate bowl and then add to the persimmon mixture.

Cover tightly with parchment paper and secure with a rubber band. Then cover dish with aluminum foil. Place on rack in a large pot and add water until it comes halfway up to the mold. Cover, bring to a boil, then lower heat and simmer for 2½ hours, adding water if necessary.

Remove mold from pot and uncover pudding; it should spring back when touched. Cool in mold for one hour, then run a knife around the edge and invert onto a dish. Serves 12.

Hanukkah

Cyclical based on lunar calendar:
the 25th day of the Jewish month of Kislev

"My first memory is of the brightness of light, light all around."

—Georgia O'Keeffe

Mystery Solved

Although I always spun the dreidel, the exact rules of the game were a mystery for most of my early childhood. Every year I would ask my mom, grandma, grandpa—anyone who would listen—how to play, but they would just mumble something about gambling, drop a few exotic sounding words like *gimel,* and claim they didn't remember the rules.

When I was about seven, my twin cousins from Pennsylvania moved to California. They were just a year or two older than me, and dressed alike—which I found fascinating. It was great to now have kids my own age to play with at family gatherings. They helped hide the matzoh at Passover, swam with me at my aunt's pool during the summer, and helped me sneak handfuls of cookies from the dessert table at Rosh Hashanah. But their greatest contribution to the holiday celebrations was a full working knowledge of the rules and regulations of the dreidel game.

The family always got together at Great Grandmother's house for Hanukkah. She made piles and piles of latkes. I'm sure there was other food too, but I only remember the latkes. After stuffing ourselves with potato pancakes, lighting the candles, and opening our gifts, my cousins and I stole away to a corner of the kitchen for a serious game of dreidel. The slightly older (by two minutes) of the twins explained the rules: Each player starts with five pieces of gelt (the standard issue in the plastic-mesh bags attached to our Hanukkah gifts) and tosses one piece into the pot. Players then take turns spinning the dreidel. Each of the sides of the dreidel has a Hebrew letter: *gimel, hay, nun, shem.* Depending on which letter the top lands on after it's spun, the player will win the whole pile of gelt, collect half of the pile, toss another piece into the pot, or pass to the next player. The game goes on until one player has all the gelt.

So cunningly simple! Why had my family been holding out on me all these years? The three of us played for what seemed like hours: winning, losing, eating our winnings, and getting loans to cover our losses from random relatives who walked past the game. I don't remember who eventually won or lost, but it became part of our holiday tradition for years.

57

Hanukkah

Sharing Traditions

The best Hanukkah I can remember took place in Madison, Wisconsin in 1969. My father was a graduate student at the university and we lived in a tiny apartment in the married student housing units. We had just moved and hadn't met any other Jewish families yet. So we invited our new, non-Jewish neighbors to join us for the first night of Hanukkah. They were obviously nervous about celebrating this foreign ritual, but the kids relaxed as soon as my father presented them each with a dollar for Hanukkah gelt. After loading up on my mother's latkes and applesauce, everyone felt comfortable enough to stay and hear the Hanukkah story and play a game of dreidel. Seeing Hanukkah through the eyes of our neighbors gave me a whole new appreciation for the holiday.

Saul's Hanukkah Latkes

This recipe is courtesy of Saul's Deli in Berkeley, California, the best Jewish deli west of New York City.

2 large peeled russet potatoes
I large egg
I tablespoon flour or matzo meal
salt and pepper to taste
peanut oil
apple sauce and sour cream, optional

Using largest hole of a grater, grate potatoes into a large bowl. Sprinkle flour or matzo meal over potatoes, add salt and pepper, and mix well with a fork. Break the egg into the potatoes and mix with a fork.

In a cast-iron skillet, pour enough peanut oil to make a ⅛-inch layer and heat very slowly—don't let the oil smoke. When oil is hot, spoon latke mix into oil and flatten with a spatula. Fry till golden brown, about 4 minutes, then flip over, reduce heat, and fry the other side, about 3 minutes. Drain onto paper towels and serve with apple sauce and sour cream, if desired. Serves 2.

59

Hanukkah

A Day in the Life

For a Hanukkah gift for a grandparent who lives far away, how about making a photo album or a video entitled "A Day it in the Life of [Your Name]." Go around with a camera or a camcorder and record ordinary scenes of the day—the kids eating breakfast, the family dog's silly tricks, soccer practice, Dad in his jogging suit, etc. For a photo album, write silly captions; with the camcorder, do a voice-over. End with a "Happy Hanukkah, we love you." Grandma will feel much closer.

Homemade Bubble Bath

This is something even tiny kids can make as a present. The trick is to have a pretty container to put it in and to never tell how you made it.

2 cups Ivory (or other unscented) dishwashing liquid
⅛ ounce of her favorite essential oil (vanilla is my favorite)

Drop the oil into the dishwashing liquid and let sit, covered, for 1 week. Pour into beautiful bottle, add a gift tag and ribbon, and instructions to use ¼ cup per bath. Makes 8 baths.

Snack Peas

This delightful snack, originally created for Purim, also comes from Saul's Deli in Berkeley, California. Says owner Karen Edelman, "Traditionally, intoxicating beverages are consumed during the meal for Purim and fried peas are the perfect accompaniment to a drink." However, it also makes a nice munchable as family members open their present.

olive oil
2 cups cooked chick peas, drained and towel-dried
salt and pepper to taste

Fill cast-iron skillet with 1-inch of olive oil and heat slowly. Do not allow to smoke. When hot enough, carefully drop peas into oil with a slotted spoon (be sure not to splatter yourself.) Allow to cook for 20 seconds or until crispy, and then remove with slotted spoon to a paper towel-lined bowl to drain. When excess oil is absorbed, remove to serving bowl and season with salt and pepper to taste. Serves 2-4.

61

Hanukkah

Homemade Paper

You and your family can make your own wrapping paper. Buy a roll of white butcher paper or brown kraft paper. For ease, you can purchase a couple of rubber stamps and different colored ink pads, and simply stamp out a pattern on your paper. Be careful not to smear it as you go. To make the paper even more personalized, you can make your own "rubber stamps." Cut a potato in half, carve a simple shape into the center, then cut the sides away so your center design is elevated enough to make a clear impression. Try simple shapes like hearts, stars, dots, and diamonds. For simple polka dots you can use wine corks. What's great is that each person gets to express his or her individuality. And your friends and family will also enjoy your efforts.

Lighten the Load

Don't forget this nice tradition: Women don't work while the menorah candles are burning—so get the biggest candles you can find.

Candle Symbolism

The "Festival of Lights" usually features white candles, but if you're not completely traditional, you might consider other colors, depending on what meaning you want to convey:

> **White:** spiritual truth and household purification
>
> **Green:** healing, prosperity, and luck
>
> **Red:** physical health and vigor
>
> **Yellow:** charm and confidence

Dreidel Dreams

The classic dreidel song is, of course, *"dreidel dreidel dreidel, I made you out of clay, and when you're dry and ready, oh dreidel I shall play."* But I learned from experience that the song isn't necessarily true.

My first-grade class was making projects from clay, and the janitor was going to bake them in the kiln, a mysterious fire-breathing oven he had down in the bowels of the school basement. The teacher showed us an example of how our projects would look—shiny, glazed, and hard as stone. Fabulous! We could make anything we wanted, and my little mind immediately recalled the dreidel song. How clever! Life imitates art! I will indeed make a dreidel, dreidel, dreidel out of clay, and when it was glazed, fired, and ready, I'd play with the coolest dreidel in town.

On clay day, I got my mom to unearth my blue and gold plastic dreidel from the box of holiday stuff out in the garage so I could bring it with me to school. I wanted to model my creation to exact proportions and etch out the Hebrew letters just right. At school, I methodically sculpted my masterpiece, painted it carefully with blue and gold glaze, and surrendered it to the awaiting fires of the kiln. It seemed like an eternity before the janitor emerged from the basement with our projects. I spotted my bright blue dreidel immediately. It was fantastic! Glistening in the sun, an exact ceramic copy of the plastic classic. At first I just held it in my hands, feeling the smooth surface and appreciating its heft. Surely this would spin for hours and win me all of the Hanukkah gelt. I took no chances spinning it in class, but allowed the teacher to wrap it carefully in newspaper for the walk home.

I proudly showed my mom the dreidel, she acknowledged it with the proper "oohs" and "ahhs," and got down with me

63

Hanukkah

on the floor to give it a whirl. But it didn't spin. It wobbled a bit (and I like to believe it *tried* to spin) but my beautiful dreidel pretty much just toppled over with a thud. I felt my lip quiver. The song had betrayed me!

My toy never turned me into the dreidel shark I had hoped to be, but it did become part of our annual holiday decoration, earning a place of honor on the mantle right next to the menorah.

Pine Cone Bird Feeder

This makes a great Hanukkah gift for the birds.

2 large pine cones
twine or red ribbon
hot glue gun
½ cup peanut butter
1 15-ounce package of bird seed
two bowls, one medium, one large
two mixing spoons
small screw-hooks (optional)

Take the pine cones and hot glue the twine or ribbon directly to the stem. Put the peanut butter into the medium bowl and the bird seed into the large bowl. Place a cone into the peanut butter and roll it around, pushing the peanut butter onto the cone with a mixing spoon. When it is well covered, transfer to the bird seed. Roll around, pressing the seed into the cone with the second spoon until well covered. Hang from a tree limb. Makes 2.

The Hiding Place

Hanukkah

One year, a few days before the holiday, my older sister and I discovered "the hiding place." In the bottom of the linen closet were huge toy bags containing two sets of identical presents—a Barbie, Ken, and Barbie house for each of us. It was a dream come true, and we could barely contain ourselves until the first night. I have long since passed on the Barbies to my children, but the memory of that Hanukkah will stay with me forever.

Holiday Napkin Rings

Here's a project kids can help with as they are getting antsy pre-dinner. It can be modified for any holiday by the kind of wrapping paper you use: red, white, and blue for 4th of July; Star of David for Hanukkah; etc.

2 empty toilet paper rolls
utility knife or x-acto knife
scissors
glue
festive wrapping paper

Take the toilet paper rolls and carefully cut them into 1½-inch width sections with the utility knife. (Measure from an end and make four marks around the roll as a guide.) You will now have six rings. Take the wrapping paper and cut it into 6 4-by-6-inch rectangles. Put glue on the back of the paper and wrap one rectangle around each ring, tucking and overlapping on the inside. Makes 6 napkin rings.

Easy Ideas for Making Hanukkah Special

- Have kids make a Star of David ornament. Cut out two equilateral triangles from a piece of cardboard. Glue one triangle on top of the other to create a six-pointed star. Spray-paint gold on front and back and, after drying, punch a hole at the top point. Tie a beautiful ribbon at the top for hanging.

- Going to someone else's house for the holiday? Bring menorah candles bundled together and tied with a beautiful blue ribbon, or one that has a Star of David pattern.

- Decorate a shoebox to house your children's dreidel collection.

- Make homemade Hanukkah cards for relatives who live far away. Little kids can draw a picture, bigger ones can add a note as well.

- You can make your own candles for your menorah—simply buy sheets of beeswax and a set of cotton wicks (available at craft stores). All you have to do is wrap the wax around the wick.

67

Hanukkah

Apricot Rugelach

What is Hanukkah without this delectable treat? My kids don't like nuts, so this version is our family favorite. The trick is to construct them while the dough is really cold because it is less sticky, so start making them the day before you want them. From there, it's a breeze.

Dough

4 ounces cream cheese, softened
⅓ cup butter, softened
¼ cup firmly packed brown sugar
¼ teaspoon salt
1 large egg yolk
1½ cups all-purpose flour

Filling

½ cup apricot preserves
½ cup dried apricots, diced

Topping

white from 1 large egg, lightly beaten
1½ tablespoons sugar

First make the dough: with an electric mixer, beat cream cheese, butter, brown sugar, salt, and egg yolk until light and fluffy. Add the flour, a little at a time, with beater on low. Divide dough in half. On a floured surface, shape each half into a ½-inch thick circle. Wrap each half separately in plastic wrap and refrigerate overnight.

Preheat oven to 350°F, and grease a cookie sheet. In a small saucepan, combine the filling ingredients and simmer until thickened.

On a floured surface, roll out 1 dough circle to 10-inches diameter. Trim so that it is even around. Spread half the filling on top. Cut into 16 wedges. Using a spatula, remove one wedge. Starting at wide end, roll up to point. Continue until you have 32 rolled up wedges.

Place rugelach point side down on cookie sheet. Brush each with egg white and sprinkle with sugar. Bake 15 minutes or until lightly browned. Makes 32.

The Mink Coat

It is summertime, that time of the year to start preparing Harvey for Hanukkah. I decide that this year I *am* going to get that Black Diamond full-length mink I have always wanted. So, I tell Harvey the size and color (so he won't get it wrong) and even take him up to the store and show him the coat I want. I say to him, "Got it? Any questions?" "No," he replies, and we go home.

I remind him a few more times (approximately once a month till December). For sure he knows what I want. I tell my mom and kids what Harvey is getting me this year. They smirk. You see, Harvey has always been a practical buyer always buying the things you need, not the things you dream of. For example, the gold watch I wanted for years turned into an everyday, expandable Timex, because it was practical. But I was sure *this time* he would get it right.

Well anyway, it's now Hanukkah, my mom is over for latkes and celebration, and the kids are real excited. Of course, no one is more excited than I am, because I am going to get a *Black Diamond full-length mink coat!* I put on the Hanukkah tape of songs to get in the spirit of things and the kids light the menorah and we start with my mom's gift, a new dress watch. Next come Jonathan's and Steven's gifts,

69

Hanukkah

a new computer with several programs—something they had wanted for a long time. Then I give Harvey his present. I had a new wedding band made for him with two diamonds (after all, I had to be grateful, I was getting a *mink coat*). He loved it. He said it was not necessary. I smiled.

Then it was my turn. Harvey went into the other room and came back with a box about seven inches long and four inches deep. Panic crept into my head, my heart stopped, and this terrible headache began to appear out of nowhere. I held the box and figured it was a hint as to where my mink coat was. I opened it up and inside sat an EpiLady razor. You heard right! You know the one, from the company that went out of business because the electric razor that was the craze that year was ripping apart women's legs and making them bleed. Everyone was returning them. Only my husband was buying one.

The first thing that enters my mind is death: how will I kill him? But the jail decor just doesn't fit my idea of chic. That won't work. My mother and kids were silent. I turn to Harvey and asked, "Where is my *coat*?" He says, "Well, I thought about it and decided to get you this razor instead so that you will stop using mine." Practical, huh? Well, I was so angry at him, the next day I returned the razor and went to the fur store and bought myself a coyote jacket.

Over the years though, I have gotten a lot of pleasure out of remembering that day. There are so many memories that my husband Harvey has given me, but this one always comes to mind with a smile. (By the way, I am still waiting for the mink. This year we are celebrating our thirtieth wedding anniversary. We will see. . . .)

71

Matzo Brie

I know, I know, this is traditionally served at Passover. But I loved it so much as a child that I would also beg for it at all the other Jewish holidays. And my mother was a soft touch—she made me Matzo Brie for breakfast every day during Hanukkah. Matzo Brie is really delicious. Fried in butter and slathered with cinnamon sugar and maple syrup, kids and adults love it, and it's so easy to make. Try making it with your children. You don't have to wait for Passover—and you don't have to be Jewish to enjoy it.

Hanukkah

3 matzo
boiling water
2 eggs, lightly beaten
salt and pepper to taste
2 tablespoons butter, margarine, or chicken fat
cinnamon sugar, honey, or maple syrup to taste

Break the matzo into bite-sized pieces and soak it in boiling water for 15 minutes. Drain and squeeze dry. Place the matzo in a bowl and add the eggs, salt, and pepper.

In a frying pan, melt the butter, margarine, or chicken fat. Taking tablespoonfuls of batter at a time, fry it in the butter. When browned on one side, turn and fry on the other side. Serve with cinnamon sugar, honey, or maple syrup. Serves 2.

72

Silly Fun

My husband and I have no kids and we're into living as simply as possible—no TV, riding our bikes rather than driving, shopping at the local food co-op, etc. But every Hanukkah, we do give each other the traditional seven nights of gifts—each a small, fun item, the sum total of which can't cost more than $35. The biggest hit so far was the year he gave me a pair of plastic fish lures as earrings; they still create a stir whenever I wear them (although some of the gag ties I've gotten him come in a close second). We open our gifts and laugh, thoroughly enjoying ourselves.

Winter Solstice

December 21

Well, it's a marvelous night
for a moondance . . .

—Van Morrison

Yule Customs

Yule is the name given to the winter solstice, the longest night of the year—a time to contemplate birth, death, and renewal. The winter solstice marks the beginning of the change from short to long days, and is celebrated with many pagan customs, including decorating with mistletoe, since mistletoe grows atop the sacred oak, the point nearest the sun; and the Yule Log, the sacred fire that burns throughout the night as a beacon and a welcome to the returning sun.

The Night of No Lights

I never knew what winter solstice was, but it has become a regular event in my house. It started twelve years ago when a buddy and I had gone skiing over Christmas vacation and were staying in his parents' cabin up in the Rockies. A particularly severe snowstorm swept through and took out the electricity. As we stumbled around in the dark searching for candles, my friend commented that this was a particularly appropriate way to spend the winter solstice and so began a tradition I have grown to cherish. We spent that evening huddled around the fireplace, telling each other stories about how we imagined our "ancestors" must have felt so many hundreds and thousands of years before the discovery of electricity.

For someone raised in the bright lights of the twentieth century, it was quite a revelation just to think about what it must have felt like throughout that vast expanse of our history when the longest night of the year was not only cold and dark, but fraught with all kinds of foreboding—what if it just kept getting darker and colder? There must have been a time when our ancestors weren't all so certain the winter would inevitably unfold into another spring.

75

Winter Solstice

We made up some pretty wild stories, but I suspect none approached how terrifying it had felt thousands of years ago. That was the first time I can remember really thinking about myself within a larger framework. The next day the lights came back on and life went on pretty much as usual, but ever since I have celebrated the winter solstice with nothing but candles and a fire. It has turned out to be a much anticipated evening.

When I introduced my soon-to-be wife to the occasion, she took to it with enthusiasm and it became a very special time for us—outside our everyday lives, outside all the trappings large and small that have come to make up who we think we are. The first couple of years together it was pretty romantic, but it evolved each year into something else. It may sound funny, but in an odd way it has become a one-night family retreat, when the things we end up discussing always surprise me.

As our children arrived, they really took to the evening. At first they just loved the idea of staying up late, sitting in the dark cuddled up with mom and dad staring at the fireplace. But as they have grown they have come to participate in their own fashion. One year, I had just finished relaying a dream I'd had and my six-year-old son started telling us his dreams. It turned out he's been having these really vivid dreams for a long time and neither of us had a clue.

Some years it's a very quiet evening, almost as if the absence of electricity makes us talk softer and slower. Other years it's a very highly charged time as if our own energy is making up for the lack of kilowatts. Last year, we even ended up with a sleep-over group of six of my daughter's most inti-mate friends giggling through the night in front of the fire-place. No matter how it develops, the winter solstice is always one of the more enjoyable days of the year.

Old-Fashioned Rice Pudding

Here's a warming treat for any cold winter's night, but especially good for solstice. And it couldn't be easier to make.

3½ cups milk
½ cup sugar, divided
½ teaspoon cinnamon
½ cup long-grain rice
2 egg yolks
½ cup whipping cream
1 teaspoon vanilla

Heat milk, ¼ cup sugar, and cinnamon in saucepan just to boil; stir in rice and reduce heat to low. Cover and simmer 35-45 minutes. In a separate bowl, whisk egg yolks, cream, ¼ cup sugar, and vanilla. Add gradually to rice. Bring to a boil and cook, stirring, for 3 minutes longer. Makes 4 servings.

77

Winter Solstice

Decorating for Yule

According to *A Druid's Herbal*, plants are brought into the house at the time of the winter solstice to assure the woodland spirits that they can find refuge during this period of darkness and cold. Plants that are brought in at this time include:

1. Yellow cedar (arborvitae) for cleansing and purity.

2. Ash, considered an herb of the sun, for protection.

3. Bay laurel, to bring the light of the sun into the house and to ward off illness.

4. Blessed thistle, an herb still used to cleanse the blood, for protection, joy, and prosperity.

5. Chamomile, an herb still used for its ability to soothe and cleanse, for love and purification.

6. Frankincense, an antiseptic herb, used symbolically to bring purification and protection.

7. Holly, for protection and to symbolize the coexistence of human and plant spirit and life.

8. Juniper, for love and protection.

9. Mistletoe, for healing, peace, and beautiful dreams.

10. Pine, for peace, healing, and joy.

Favorite Holiday

I grew up in the lush green environs of the Pacific Northwest, so we were hardly lacking for trees, but it was family tradition to augment the number on an annual basis for the

Christmas holiday season—my parents, strict environmentalists, had a "no cut policy." Instead, we would plant a tree. And what a production it was! All four of us kids would pile into the Country Squire (we always had to "choose" who got to ride in the back-facing jump seat), and head to Rutherford's Nursery, my dad's one-stop shop for all his gardening needs. There, disagreement would frequently ensue. Would we plant a fir this year? Evergreen, but they take so long to grow. Something traditional, like an oak or an elm? Boring! A flowering tree? (That was always Mom's preference.) In the end, we would find something that seemed to work well, and we would head back home. Having visited California's legendary redwood groves on family driving trips, for me the tree always represented mysterious perpetuity and a kind of cosmic power—who knew what would happen to us as this tree stood quietly growing over two or three hundred years? As a third-grade teacher, I've begun sending my students home every winter solstice with a little seedling to plant; it always reminds me of the Native American proverb: "We do not inherit the earth from our grandparents. We borrow it from our children."

79

Winter Solstice

Spicy Bath Salts

Looking for an easy-to-make natural treat for a teacher or friend? Try these fabulous bath salts. They will be greatly appreciated.

2 cups kosher salt
1 attractive glass jar with tight-fitting lid
2 large handfuls pine needles

Place 2 tablespoons salt evenly on the bottom of the jar. Lay 12 pine needles over the salt. Alternate salt and pine needles until the jar is full. Cover and place in a cool dark spot for four to six weeks. Add a pretty ribbon and gift tag. Makes 1 jar.

A Personal Ritual

For winter solstice, I like to be with my family sitting around the table and drinking many hot beverages—especially apple cider—and eating spiced breads. For my ritual, I burn candles and say a prayer to the Great Bear of the North (Indian legend) even though I am Dutch/English by origin. The response draws me outdoors where I observe the moon, now full in all its splendor. I thank God for the time.

Wassail Through the Night

One Yule tradition is wassailing. Wassail is an alcoholic drink made of cider or ale. In the past, it was placed in a wooden bowl and carried door to door throughout the neighborhood, gathering people to drink, sing, and spread tidings of good cheer.

In the British Isles, folks not only "wassail" one another, but the trees. A tree is chosen, usually an oak, and a hymn is sung to it, wishing it good health and long life. A blessing is also bestowed upon it to be fruitful; then guns are fired or some other loud noise is made in order to drive off any bad spirits. People then drink toasts to the tree and some wassail is poured on the earth around the trunk while bread and cakes are placed upon its branches.

81

Winter Solstice

Wassail

In modern times, wassail is usually served indoors, at holiday parties. This recipe, which can be nonalcoholic, is from the Wedgewood Inn in New Hope, Connecticut.

I gallon apple cider
2 quarts cranberry juice
I tablespoon whole allspice

2 oranges, studded with cloves
4 sticks cinnamon
2 cups rum, optional

In a 2-gallon pot combine all ingredients and heat gently. Serve warm. Makes 24 servings.

Easy Ideas for Celebrating Yule

- Decorate a tree in your yard with candycanes or homemade stars covered in aluminum foil. Make sure you use lots of lights!

- String popcorn and cranberries in a tree or bush as a treat for the birds and squirrels.

- Bring as much greenery (holly, mistletoe, evergreens) into your home as you can to remind yourself that life goes on even in the darkest of times.

- On solstice night, gather candles and matches and then turn off all the lights in your home. After dwelling on the dark for a few moments, light the candles and welcome the light back into the world.

- Spicing up the flames: sprinkle a few drops of frankincense, cedarwood, or pine essential oil onto a log before lighting it and you will enjoy an even more fragrant fire.

The Yule Log

The second week in December, we always go out to the woodpile to find the biggest log to burn on winter solstice, December 21. We carry it into the house, place it on the hearth, and then decorate it with a beautiful ribbon and sprigs of fresh rosemary from our garden. Rosemary is the symbol of friendship and remembrance. On the solstice, we gather together in front of the fireplace, burn the log, and celebrate being together again. Traditionally, the Yule Log was brought into an outdoor clearing to become part of a great bonfire. Everyone would dance and sing around the fire. All the noise and great excitement is said to awaken the sun from its long winter sleep, hurrying spring on its way. Because we don't have the space for a safe outdoor fire, we always do it indoors, hoping it will have the same effect on the sun. We're careful not to let the log burn completely, so we'll have little bits left over to give to all our friends to start the next day's fires in their own hearths.

83

Winter Solstice

Ah, the Sun

Two years ago I lived in Florida, and never thought about the solstice or even knew when it occurred. Now I live in Alaska, and I count the days! In December, the sun barely clears the mountains, and then only hovers weakly, casting a pale light for a few hours. I think about all the daily chores I need to do, and I want to go back to bed! I feel as tired and unenergetic as the feeble sunlight. Winter solstice is an important part of life here—spiritually for some, physically and mentally for all. As we await whatever winter holiday we celebrate, we also anticipate the return of light, warmth, and energy.

Christmas Eve

*How many old recollections, and how many
dormant sympathies, does Christmas time awaken!
Happy, happy Christmas ... that can recall to
the old man the pleasures of his youth; that can transport
the sailor and the traveler, thousands of miles away,
back to his own fireside and his quiet home!*

—Charles Dickens

A Fun Tradition

We have a tradition in my family of saying "Christmas Eve Gift" to the first family member whom we see that evening. That person must give you a gift of some sort. It's a fun way to get the festivities going.

Jingle All the Way

On Christmas Eve when my kids were little and it was late at night, I used to run around outside jingling bells under their windows. They would go wild with excitement!

Can't Wait

Christmas Eve was always hard on me as a kid because I couldn't wait for Santa to come. Then my mom hit on a tradition that we have done every year since that helps with the wait. Every Christmas Eve she lets my brother and me open one present. Then we drive around town to look at all the lights. It's a great way to spend the evening.

The Christmas Angel

Every December 24, we lay out the Christmas tree star on the table before the kids go to bed. When they are asleep, the Christmas Angel comes in and puts up the star and lights the tree. My kids look forward to this almost as much as they do to the arrival of Santa.

87

Christmas Eve

The Guest of Honor

My family shares a special tradition on Christmas Eve. A place is reserved for all at the dinner table with one extra, vacant place set aside for the Guest of Honor, who is the reason for the celebration. The table is decorated in white lace with white candles. We place several pieces of bread wafer on a small dish at the center of the table. Before dinner, each family member takes his or her share of the wafer and breaks a piece with every other member of the family, giving each other a hug and kiss; we all wish each other a very happy Christmas and healthy New Year. Then we sit down for a big Polish dinner, eat until we nearly burst, drink until we're goofy, and laugh about all of the weird things we'd done throughout our lives. It is indeed the best day of the year.

Blending Traditions

One of my favorite holidays is Christmas Eve, because we have most of the family together, celebrating with influences from both my dad's and mom's ancestries. For the Italian side, we have a seafood feast, with shrimp, clams, calamari, and scallops over pasta. It's a traditional Italian "feast of the seven seafoods," the meaning of which I don't know. And we obviously don't follow it to a tee, as we don't have seven seafoods. But the preparation is a big to-do, with my dad and the guys in the family shucking the clams, my mom and sisters frying the shrimp, me sautéing the scallops, and kids running around all over the place.

But the most special part of the dinner is my mom's Polish tradition of the *oplatki* or Christmas wafer. Everyone gets a square of this wafer. We all go around to each other and as one person takes a tiny piece of the wafer and eats it, the other person wishes something special for that person, such as good health, happiness, and prosperity. Or you can wish something specific, such as good luck in finding a new job, or sanity during wedding plans, etc. Our family's gotten so big (the immediate family is thirty-seven!), that now we just stand in a circle and offer one general wish to everyone, with special wishes to specific individuals as desired. As kids, we used to make fun of my mom because she would always cry during this ceremony, but now, as we adults realize how special and loving and wonderful this little offering is, tears are shed throughout the whole room.

Then, after the huge meal, we open presents for a few hours. Given the number of us, with the majority being young children, one can guess how chaotic this process is! But it's all fun.

89

Christmas Eve

Car Caroling

Even though I moved three states away from home after college, nothing could keep me away from my best friend and my mom at Christmas time. After Christmas Eve Mass, we would go "car caroling." We'd roll down the windows, and belt out "Jingle Bells" at the top of our lungs. We'd just drive in the fresh northern winter air, singing our favorite tunes and being together. It made Christmas perfect.

Easy Ideas for Caroling

If you want to do something a bit more formal than car caroling, consider the following for making it a special occasion:

- Bring people together a half hour early for practice.
- Have a sheet with lyrics for everyone.
- Don't forget flashlights.
- Consider singing at a nursing home or homeless shelter.
- Finish back at your house with hot chocolate and cookies!

Hot Buttered Rum

Here's a Christmas tradition, perfect for after caroling.

1 teaspoon brown sugar
2 ounces rum
4 ounces (½ cup) hard cider
1 tablespoon butter
a pinch of grated nutmeg

Combine sugar and rum in a mug or glass. Over medium heat, warm cider to a pre-boil, then add butter, stirring until melted. Pour into mug, and serve immediately, dusted with nutmeg. Serves 1.

The Kindness Box

Leading up to the holidays, we have a kindness box. We wrap up a shoebox like a present and cut a slot in the top. We put the box and a pencil and some paper under the tree. When someone in the family notices someone being kind, we write the act down on a piece of paper and put it in the box. (Young children could draw a picture or tell Mom what they saw and ask her to write it down.) On Christmas Eve, along with reading a beautiful picture book of the Christmas story, we open the box and read all the notes.

91

Christmas Eve

Magic Reindeer Food

Here's a great inexpensive gift idea for Brownie leaders, teachers, and anyone elses. Or you can just make it for your kids. I fill a Ziploc baggie with about 1 teaspoon of red and green glitter and ¼ cup of instant oatmeal. I then attach a xeroxed picture of a reindeer and the following saying: "On Christmas Eve, sprinkle this Magic Reindeer Food on your lawn. The Magic Glitter sparkling in the moonlight and the smell of oats will guide Rudolf to your home." To make it even cuter, I glue a red pom-pom to the reindeer's nose. It's always been a hit with everyone I've sent it to. Remember to sweep up the oats after the kids have gone to bed because they will ask the next morning why Rudolf didn't eat them.

Unique Tradition

When I was about eight, my family decided to create family traditions to have each year on Christmas Eve. My mom would cook a Christmas Eve dinner, my dad would read from Luke and *The Night Before Christmas*. When it got to me, all the good ones were taken! So, I thought really hard and came up with—a bubble-gum blowing contest. It has little to do with our Savior's birth but we always laugh and have a great time. Now it's one of the most important parts of Christmas for me.

Sleeping in the Glow

My husband and I have a Christmas tradition of sleeping in the living room, in front of the Christmas tree, on Christmas Eve. It's wonderful to fall asleep surrounded by the colorful glow of Christmas lights and the fresh, piney smell. One of my favorite things to do is put on my husband's glasses (he's blind as a bat) and see the tree as a big blob of psychedelic light bursts. One year we snuggled up on the foam futon that was our bed each December 24, expecting the usual visions of dancing sugar plums. As soon as our heads hit the pillow, we knew the visions would be slightly more nightmarish. John's eyes started watering profusely, and my throat seized up so tight I was afraid I might stop breathing if I fell asleep. The futon had become infested with some hideous strain of mold since we had put it away the previous year. Gasping and teary, we tossed the foul furniture outside and spent the night in our regular bed. The moral of the story? Make it a simple pleasure of two or three of the other holidays of the year to air out the futon!

93

Christmas Eve

Christmas

December 25

For somehow, not only at Christmas,
but all the long year through,
the joy that you give to others
is the joy that comes back to you.

—John Greenleaf Whittier

The Christmas Pledge

Last year, everyone in my family took the Christmas pledge as described in the book *Unplug the Christmas Machine*. It goes like this: "Believing in the beauty and simplicity of Christmas, I commit myself to the following:

1. To remember those people who truly need my gifts.

2. To express my love for family and friends in more direct ways than presents.

3. To rededicate myself to the spiritual growth of my family.

4. To examine my holiday activities in light of the true spirit of Christmas.

5. To initiate one act of peacemaking within my circle of family and friends.

Papier-Mâché Flower Vase

Here's a gift an older child can make.

I cup flour
¾ cup cold water

1-by-8-inch strips of newspaper
clean, empty round salad dressing bottle
1 can white spray paint
colored paint of your choice
paint brush
spray sealer
ribbons, glitter, sequins, optional
hot-glue gun, optional

Mix the flour and water in a bowl until it's smooth. Take the strips of newspaper and dip them into the paste. Make sure both sides of the strip are covered. Place the strips onto the bottle, two layers thick, smoothing each strip as you go along. If necessary, you may want to place one extra strip around the threads at the mouth of the bottle. Let sit for a couple of days until it has completely dried.

Spray the white paint on the bottle so the newspaper is completely covered. This may take two or three coatings. When dry, paint the bottle the color you have chosen or paint designs on the white background. When dry, spray with the clear sealer. If you want to add decorative items such as ribbon, beads, or glitter, hot-glue them to the bottle.

The Christmas Tree

There was no way we were not going to have a Christmas tree. It was going to be Juan Miguel's second Christmas in this country, and like every eight-year-old, he was full of expectations about how his home should be that December.

I had just abruptly cut ties with a previous employer—and Juan Miguel's father, who had arrived with him from the Philippines a little over a year earlier, had only been at work a few months. We were not, however, going to allow our shaky finances to shun the holiday spirit.

Were we, therefore, going to settle for a potted, twelve-inch, drugstore-variety tree? Or a practical plastic facsimile that would outlive, hopefully, our unemployed days?

We went for neither. We drove to the lot and, with Juan's approval, came away with a six-foot Scotch pine.

The tree was just right for our one-room apartment, perfuming the entire space with its holiday scent. It was time to hang up the pink butterfly mobiles my mother had sent me from Manila the year before. These handmade beauties did more than stir my aesthetic senses. They were handcrafted by indigent folks employed by the daughter of one of the Philippines' best-loved nationalists. Having received them after February 1986, the year Filipinos waged their successful peaceful revolution, the butterflies signified my native land's liberation from despotism.

Even with the diaphanous wonders, the tree left much to be desired. Our situation called for creativity. I turned away from ersatz holly and berry mingled with glistening garlands that I couldn't afford. Deep examination of conscience told me to take two rolls of illusion tulle which would make a nest, one each, for the bundle of pink poinsettias, marked 75 percent off. I could make enough nested flowers for a quarter of what it would have cost me to have a handful of ready-made ornaments.

Our tree looked different, all right. So unique that Juan Miguel, already beginning to feel the weight of peer pressure, wondered why it didn't "look happy like all other Christmas trees" with the red, green, and gold trimmings. Individualism, I assured him, was good.

Thirteen years later, look who gushes each time he beholds our tree. Somehow, it seems taller, brighter, closer to perfection each year, bringing the widest smiles from its handmaidens.

When we look at the formidable fir in our living room now, we see more than a symbol of a season. We seen whence and where we've come, and how truly blessed we are.

99

Christmas

The True Christmas Spirit

This holiday season, check out The North Pole Christmas Mission (www.thenorthpole.com). Here, kids can write letters to Santa and share ideas of things to do in the season of giv-ing. Here are some of the suggestions found on this Website:

- Take time out during this busy holiday season to read a holiday story to someone in your family. Not only will you enjoy it, they'll remember it as one of their most special holiday moments of this year!

- I think that all kids should take plates of cookies to the old people in their neighborhood 'cause sometimes they don't get to see their families.

- Write your loved ones a Christmas message and give them a hug after they're done reading it.

- I cleaned out my coat closet and gave lots of warm things to people who need it.

Bow Sachets

Here's a great Christmas present that uses lace trim scraps. You can either buy potpourri or make your own; the recipe follows.

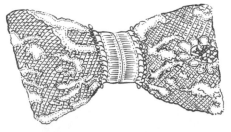

1 3-inch wide scrap of lace trim,
finished on both edges
1 3-inch wide scrap of fine tulle
thread to match
potpourri
1 inch wide moire ribbon

Cut a length of lace trim about 4 inches long. Place the tulle, cut to fit, on wrong side of lace and stitch along the two long and one short edge. Turn right side out and fill loosely with potpourri. Wrap the ribbon tightly around the center of the pouch, overlapping ends at back. Tuck under cut edge of ribbon and stitch it in place. Makes 1 sachet.

Christmas

Rose Potpourri

This is a real treat for rose lovers.

½ teaspoon rose essential oil
1½ tablespoons orris root (available at herb
stores and from catalogs)
2 cups dried rose petals
2 cups dried rose geranium leaves

Combine the oil and orris root and let sit for a few days. Add to the flowers and leaves and stir well. Keep it in covered container until ready to use. Makes 4 cups.

Potpourri Supplies

If you are having trouble finding the ingredients to make all the wonderful potpourri recipes in this book, write: Lavender Lane, P.O. Box 7265, Citrus Heights, CA 95621 ($2 for catalog); Rosemary House, 120 South Market Street, Mechanicsburg, PA 17055 ($2 for catalog); or Indiana Botanic Gardens, P.O. Box 5, Hammond, IN 46325 (free).

Old-Fashioned Fun

When I was a kid, we always used to make snowflakes by folding white paper and then cutting out intricate patterns with scissors. Then we'd Scotch-tape them onto the front windows. We also used to love to make "stained glass windows" by ironing crayon shavings between two sheets of waxed paper until the colors melted and ran together. These would be hung in the windows also. Now that I have children, they have begun to look forward to making these simple decorations each December.

Scented Ornaments

Here's another wonderful and simple decorating idea. No, they are not edible!

1 4-ounce can ground cinnamon (about 1 cup)
1 tablespoon ground cloves
1 tablespoon ground nutmeg
¾ cup applesauce
2 tablespoons white glue
thread
glitter glue, fabric, or other decorating items, optional

103

Christmas

In a medium bowl, combine cinnamon, cloves, and nutmeg. Add applesauce and glue; stir to combine. Work mixture with hands 2 to 3 minutes or until dough is smooth and ingredients are thoroughly mixed. Divide dough into 4 portions. Roll out each dough portion to ¼-inch thickness. Cut dough with cookie cutters. Using a toothpick, make small hole through the top of each ornament. Place cut-out ornaments on wire rack to dry. Allow several days to dry, turning ornaments over once a day. Create hangers by pushing a length of thread through the hole at the top of each one. Decorate as desired with glitter, beads, or fabric, or use as is.

A Box of Memories

After my first child was born, I started a Christmas tradition that has been a lot of fun. Every Christmas I give each child a special ornament towards a collection that they can take with them when they leave home to begin setting up their own homes. That way, they can take some "Christmas memories" with them.

The Little Things

When I was growing up, my favorite part of Christmas was the stocking. The stocking was like the icing on the cake—we always opened them last, after all the other gifts had been given. Santa was very practical at our house; the stockings were filled with shampoo, underwear, toilet water, and the like, and they always had a navel orange in the toe and a big fat candy cane stuck on the top. I'm not even a big fan of candy canes, but I always looked forward to it. I would peel the orange, stick the candy cane in the center, and savor the two tastes blending together in my mouth.

Natural Stockings

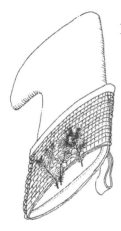

Make a unique Christmas stocking for your loved ones. Simply buy a plain red stocking and a 5-inch wide piece of rug-hooking mesh (available at needlecraft stores). Sew the mesh to the stocking and then tuck small bits of evergreen branches or colored leaves into the mesh.

Christmas

Candy Cane Potpourri

If you are a fan more of the scent than the taste of peppermint, consider this holiday potpourri.

4 cups dried peppermint leaves
3 cups dried pink rose petals and buds
1 cup dried hibiscus flowers
1 tablespoon whole cloves
1 tablespoon broken pieces of cinnamon sticks
2 tablespoons orris root (available at herbal stores and from catalogs)
20 drops rose essential oil
10 drops peppermint essential oil
1 tablespoon gum benzoin (available at herbal stores and from catalogs)

Combine all ingredients except gum benzoin and stir well. Add gum benzoin and stir well again. Makes 2 quarts.

The Little Christmas Star

When I was in the sixth grade, my teacher decided to have a Christmas Lantern contest. Lanterns are a part of the traditional celebration of Christmas in the Philippines. They are usually made of bamboo split into thin sticks to make the frame which is usually in the form of a star and covered with tissue paper. Sometimes, we put a candle or light bulb inside and hang them by the window. My sixth-grade teacher challenged us to make the prettiest lantern to bring to class.

I was frantic because I did not have tissue paper. But I did have plenty of white typewriting paper which my uncle provided. I made glue out of rice and went to the woods to gather bamboo for the frame. Needless to say, I produced the smallest white star lantern with streamers. One streamer was slightly torn, but I was proud of it so I brought it to school the next day. My teacher hung it up amidst all the dazzling huge stars with colorful streamers.

And there it was, almost invisible until the day when the nuns from the town's convent came to teach us our weekly catechism. They "oohed" and "ahhhed" at all the lanterns.

Suddenly, they pointed to my little star, asking who made it. My teacher told them it was me. The good sisters put their heads together as if in prayer, then motioned for me to come. I have always been scared of them because of their black habits blowing in the wind, so I went reluctantly. Then they asked me if I would sell them my star. Dumbfounded, I said yes! They offered me 50 cents and I was so happy, thinking I could now buy my brothers' Christmas presents without having to make them. (I did not win the lantern contest that day, but I did not care. A lantern made of rose and blue tissues won and I knew in my heart that the father of my classmate deserved the award.)

The nuns went back to the convent happy with their purchase, I stopped at the country store and bought bath soap, a comb, and candies to give to my brothers as presents. And for me, I bought a small Santa Claus I'd been eyeing for weeks. It was made of twisted red and white chenille. I didn't give my little white star another thought.

Christmas morning came and my mother brought us all to church in town. As I glanced upward to receive the Host, I saw something that brought joy to my heart. Up on the altar above the Nativity hung my little white star! I knew it was the one the nuns bought from me because of the twisted point and torn streamer. This happened to me a long time ago, but I will always cherish the memories of that Christmas day.

107

Christmas

Personally Scented Candles

You can make your own homemade scented candles for your home and as gifts. They are incredibly easy to make—you just need to plan in advance. The fragrance will be released as they burn. (If you haven't planned ahead, you can still get some of the effect by sprinkling a drop or two of your favorite essential oil in the melted wax of a plain candle as it burns.)

2 ounces of your favorite essential oil
(or try a combination—vanilla and rose are
my personal favorites for romance)
¼ cup orris root powder (available at herbal stores)
1 large, airtight plastic container big enough to fit candles
6 unscented candles, any size

Combine the oil(s) and the orris root and sprinkle in the bottom of the container. Place candles inside, cover, and store in a cool spot for 4 to 6 weeks.

Easy Ideas for Making Christmas Manageable

- If loved ones are far away, record your family singing carols and send them a tape.

- Agree to a scaled-down event among the group of people you normally exchange gifts with. Place everyone's name in a hat and pick one. You get a gift only for that person. Or at least agree to a spending limit among family members.

- Secret Santas at work—same thing—one gift under $10.

- Don't overload kids with gifts. Too many and they turn into greedy monsters, and you are in the poorhouse. My sister keeps presents back from her daughter (she's loaded with overindulgent aunts and uncles) and doles them out throughout the year.

- Shop throughout the year and find a good hiding place to stash your loot. You'll save money (no last-minute impulse purchases) and aggravation. And don't forget the day after Christmas sales of cards, wrapping paper, and decorations.

109

Christmas

Picasso Pillow

Here's a great one-of-a-kind gift that older kids can do on their own or that younger kids can make with help to show off their artistic prowess.

I drawing
I pillow-sized piece of foam
2 pieces of plain fabric, each an inch larger around than the foam
tracing paper
liquid embroidery (available at craft stores)
needle and thread

Find a piece of art that the child has done and likes. Trace it onto one of the pieces of fabric. Using the liquid embroidery, embroider the lines of the drawing onto the fabric. Place the two pieces of fabric together inside out and sew on three sides. Insert the foam and stitch the fourth side.

Gift of Love

The best gift I ever received came from my grandmother last year. She decided that she wanted to live to see her family enjoy their "inheritances." I was overwhelmed when I found out that she had left me her wedding and engagement rings. Not only do I have a constant reminder of her love, but also of my grandfather's love. Whenever I look at the diamond as it sparkles in the engagement ring, I see the twinkle in my grandfather's eyes and feel his love coming to me all the way from Heaven.

Mistletoe Ball

Instead of a little sprig of mistletoe in your doorway, how about hanging a beautiful kissing ball? It's easy.

1 6-inch wide ball of floral foam
chicken wire, the same size as the foam
decorative cord or ribbon for hanging the ball
various evergreens such as pine, holly, hemlock
mistletoe

Soak the floral foam in water until thoroughly wet. Wrap the foam in the wire and tie the ribbon or cord of desired length to the chicken wire. Insert small pieces of greens into the foam to create a pleasing circular shape. Insert mistletoe at the base of circle so it hangs lower than the rest of the greens. Hang in doorway.

111

Christmas

Gilded Angel

I have been a collector of angels since before it became a craze. This is one of my favorites, because it is so easy to make. I made several for my house and gave some away as gifts. They look great all year round. The supplies are all available at craft stores and there's plenty of paint left over to make more or to gild flower pots.

I terra-cotta angel of your choice
I can gold spray paint
I I-ounce jar white acrylic craft paint
I jar clear paint thinner
I small art paintbrush

Lay old newspaper down on the surface you will be working on. Spray the angel with gold paint, covering it completely, and allow it to thoroughly dry.

In a paper cup or jar, make a mixture of ½ white paint and ½ paint thinner. Paint this on the angel, being careful not to create pools of paint in crevices. Immediately wipe the white paint off all the raised surfaces, leaving it untouched on the recessed surfaces to create an antique look. (You may need to rub quite hard.) Makes I angel.

Easy Ideas for Inexpensive Decorations

- Gather enough pine cones to have one for each person eating with you. Use them as place cards by writing each person's name on a slip of paper and tucking it into the scales of the cones.

- You can make beautiful balls of acorns, pine cones, or cran-berries for decorations or gifts. Buy some papier-mâché balls at a craft store and gather whatever items you plan to use. Using a hot-glue gun, place glue on one section of the ball, then glue pine cones, acorns, or cranberries onto the ball, as close together as possible. Continue until you've completely covered the surface. These can be displayed on your table or a sideboard.

113

Christmas

- Do you have solid-colored glass ornaments that you're tired of? Let your children turn them into one-of-a-kind family heir-looms with glitter glue and holiday stickers or craft paints.

- Core some apples and place candles inside. Place on mantle in between sections of an evergreen swag.

- Decorate your tree with all natural substances—pine cones you gathered, pyracantha or bittersweet from your yard.

- Do an ornament swap with friends.

- Try dried flowers on your tree this year—statice, caspia, baby's breath, and heather all air-dry well. Simply use floral wire to create bunches, leaving a couple of inches of wire to attach to tree. For fresh flowers, you can use those water tubes available from flower and craft stores. Insert the flower in the tube, and wrap the wire around the tube, leaving enough to attach to tree.

- Decorate your table with sugared fruit, an old-fashioned Christmas tradition. Dip apples, pears, plums, and grapes into egg white and then roll in granulated sugar. Arrange attractively in a bowl.

- Set out bowls of tangerines and oranges that you've studded with cloves for a delicious aroma.

- Decorate your tree with seashells you've collected. Starfish, sand dollars, and sea urchins can be draped on branches and tiny holes can be drilled in scallop shells so they can be hung.

- Kids love to make the old-fashioned popcorn and cranberry strings and paper chains for the tree.

- Tie family photos to the tree to bring loved ones who are far away closer.

- Save the little boxes that paper clips and toothpicks come in, and wrap them like little presents with scraps of wrapping paper and narrow ribbon.

- Make lace napkin rings for your cloth napkins. Nothing could be easier. Simply roll the napkins and tie with 24 inches of 1-inch wide lace. Trim edges of the lace so they look finished.

Christmas Joys

As a child, Christmas was one of my favorite times of year. First and foremost, there were the gifts. Second, it meant a whole week out of school. And there was the annual foray to Sears with my mother and grandmother to outfit my brother and sister and me with new Sunday-go-to-meeting clothes. Sunday was always a dress-up day, but, like Easter, Christmas was special. Everyone in church showed up in their new finery: the women in hats and gloves, the little girls in ruffled dresses, nice coats, and Shirley Temple curls, the little boys miniatures of their fathers in new suits, hair slick with pomade. The sermon would be longer than usual that day, with reprimands for all those who only showed up in church on Christmas and Easter, very trying for us children (wiggling in the pews was not allowed). But it was worth the wait, for after church the family—parents, grandparents, aunts, uncles, cousins—would gather to open presents and then have dinner.

And the dinner! The warm, yeasty smell of homemade rolls rising in the kitchen; mashed potatoes; gravy made with the flavorful drippings from the roasted chickens; candied carrots; string bean casserole. But if Thanksgiving was not complete without a turkey, Christmas was not complete without

115

Christmas

a ham. Skin sliced in a criss-cross pattern, cloves in each inter-section, brown sugar and pineapple glaze, with pineapple rings on top, each one centered with a cherry. We children had dibs on the pineapple, redolent with ham juices and glaze.

The family is scattered now, some have moved, some have died, and our Christmas dinners are only sweet memories. But if I close my eyes and concentrate, I can smell those delicious aromas again and feel the joy of sharing in a special family occasion.

Holiday Ham

This is the classic recipe. If you have managed to live this long without giving it a try, rectify the situation immediately. You're guaranteed to be delighted.

1 ham, about 5 pounds
whole cloves
brown sugar
1 20-oz can pineapple slices in juice
maraschino cherries

Preheat oven to 350°F. Score the surface of ham with a knife and insert whole cloves in each intersection. Put in baking pan and bake. If ham is not precooked, allow 20 minutes per pound. If precooked, follow wrapper instructions.

Pour juice from pineapple slices into a bowl. Add enough brown sugar to make a thin paste. Baste ham with glaze every 15 minutes or so. Cover the ham with the pineapple rings approximately half an hour before ham is done (use toothpicks to hold in place if necessary) and place a cherry in the center of each pineapple slice. Serves 8.

Decorative Choker

Dressing up in all your finery is definitely a holiday tradition. This easy-to-make necklace is perfect for young girls and women of all ages.

117

Christmas

velvet ribbon
1-inch length of self-stick Velcro
(should be the same color as the ribbon)
scissors
dried flower
spray craft glaze
hot glue

Measure the neck size of the wearer. Add one inch and cut the ribbon to this size. Take the fuzzy-cloth side of the Velcro and attach it to one end of the ribbon (if the backing is not strong enough to attach to the ribbon, use a drop of hot glue.) Take the plastic side of the Velcro, cut in half. Attach this to the back side of the other end of the ribbon. Make sure when you wrap the ribbon around

the person's neck that the Velcro will catch. Take the dried flower
and spray the head with the glaze to protect it. After it has dried,
cut off the stem. Hot glue the flower to the center of the ribbon.

Flower Barrettes

plain plastic hair barrettes
small dried flowers— (mall rose buds and baby's breath are nice)
glue gun

Decide on a pleasing arrangement and hot-glue the flowers onto
the barrettes.

Tree Treat

The Saturday before Christmas, the food co-op in our town
would sell Christmas trees beginning at 7 A.M. The day of the
sale, my dad, brother, and I would get up at 5 A.M., go down
to Bette's Diner, which is so famous that even that early we
would have to wait an hour to get seated. I would always
have their fabulous pancakes and then we would hurry over
to the co-op to get there just as it opened. We would always
pick the tallest tree (our house has a twenty-two-foot ceiling),

strap it onto the car, and head for home. We would always decorate it the same day. To reach the top, we would drag the tree over to the balcony and lean over. As the youngest, I always got to put the star on top. The food co-op is gone now, and we can get our tree any old time. Somehow a bit of the magic is also gone.

119

Christmas

Stirring up Happiness

Sometime late in November, my mother would make a Christmas pudding. Everyone would help out, chopping fruit and measuring ingredients. When it was done, she put a shiny new quarter in the batter and we would all take turns to stir the mixture and make a wish for the coming new year. It was then steamed for eight hours, covered, and left in the pantry. During the month before Christmas day, she would treat it with brandy once a week. Then, on Christmas day, after the big turkey dinner, she would reheat the pudding until it was steaming, cover it in heated brandy, turn all the lights off in the dining room, set the pudding down on the table, and light the brandy. A beautiful sight! Whoever found the quarter in their piece of pudding got an extra present.

Old-Fashioned Plum Pudding

1½ pounds raisins
½ cup chopped almonds
2 ounces candied citron, finely chopped
2 cups finely diced apples
1 cup brandy
1½ cup dry bread crumbs
1 cup finely chopped suet
½ cup sugar
1 cup molasses
3 eggs
¼ cup flour
1 teaspoon cinnamon
1 teaspoon salt
½ teaspoon allspice
1/2 teaspoon cloves
rind of 1 lemon

Combine the raisins, almonds, citron, apples, and brandy, and allow to sit overnight. The next day, preheat oven to 300°F. Combine the fruit mixture with the remaining ingredients one at a time. Mix well, turn into a buttered pudding mold, and cover tightly with parchment paper secured by rubber bands. Place mold in a large roasting pan and fill pan with boiling water. Steam 7 to 8 hours—the longer the better—adding more water if necessary. To serve, loosen the side of the pudding with a knife and invert onto a serving platter. Serve with hard sauce. Serves 12.

Hard Sauce

1 cup butter
2 cups powdered sugar, sifted
1 large egg yolk
4 tablespoons heavy cream
4 tablespoons cognac

Combine the butter and confectioners' sugar. Beat in the remaining ingredients. Makes 2 cups.

121

Christmas

Old-Fashioned Toys

Are you looking for the toys from your youth for your children or grandchildren—things like wooden Tinkertoys and Lincoln Logs, Raggedy Anns, pogo sticks, American Eagle sleds, etc? Well, look no further than the Back to Basics Toys catalog. For a copy, call 800-356-5360.

Random Acts of Holiday Kindness

Having been a single mother for eight years, I know how hard it is to afford the Christmas you want to give your kids, and how far a parent will stretch to achieve this. We hit upon the idea of going to WalMart in mid-December, and paying off (or making a large payment on) someone's layaway—one with toys on it. We love the idea of someone showing up to make a payment, a payment that might mean doing without something else, and being told that their account is paid and they can take the gifts home!

122

A Natural Christmas

Looking for ecologically sound gifts with all-recycled packaging? Consider the Harmony Catalog (800-869-3446). It's packed with loads of eco-friendly tools and ideas for simple living year round.

Hydrangea Wreath

This is the height of simplicity and beauty. Buy a plain evergreen wreath (the Boy Scouts always sell them outside my local supermarket). Take five bunches of dried hydrangea blossoms and insert them in the wreath equidistant to one another. If the stems aren't long enough to secure by themselves, attach with florist's wire. Make five simple bows that complement the hues in the hydrangeas (teak blue moire silk is spectacular, but ivory or pink might also work).

Attach a bow with florist's wire to each hydrangea bunch. Hang indoors.

Cookie Delights

What is Christmas without cookies, particularly an assortment of cookies? Here's a potpourri of people's favorites; I hope you find one that will become your signature cookie.

Christmas

Gingerbread

This old-fashioned gingerbread recipe dates back to colonial New England, and is ideal for creating holiday "gingerbread people."

5 cups flour
3 cups sugar
1½ teaspoons baking soda
2 tablespoons ground ginger
1 pound butter, softened
3 eggs
1½ cups milk

Preheat oven to 375°F. Sift together flour, sugar, baking soda, and ginger. Gradually combine with butter (mixture will feel coarse and crumbly). In a separate bowl, combine the eggs and milk, then add to the flour mixture, stirring until well blended.

With a floured rolling pin, roll the dough out thinly onto a large baking sheet. Bake 5 to 10 minutes, or until brown.

Unusual Cookie Cutters

If you are looking for great cookie cutters (including a running gingerbread man and a guardian angel), great shortbread stamps, as well as hundreds of other unique holiday items and fabulous gifts, check out the Gooseberry Patch catalog (800-854-6673). It truly is loaded with one-of-a-kind delights.

Handprint Cookies

These cookies are a delight for little ones to make—and a pleasure to consume.

½ cup butter or margarine, softened

1 cup sugar

1 egg

1 cup molasses

½ cup water

7 cups flour

1 teaspoon baking soda

1 teaspoon salt

½ teaspoon ginger

½ teaspoon nutmeg
½ teaspoon allspice
½ teaspoon cloves

Mix the butter or margarine, sugar, and egg in a bowl. Blend in the molasses and water. Add remaining ingredients and mix thoroughly. Cover and refrigerate for an hour.

Preheat oven to 350°F, and grease a baking sheet. On a floured board, roll out a portion of the dough until it is ½-inch thick. Spread flour on the surface of the dough. Place a hand lightly on the surface of the dough and cut around the hand and fingers with a butter knife dipped in flour. Use a wide spatula to transfer the cookie to baking sheet. Sprinkle the cookie with sugar. Repeat using the rest of the dough. Bake for 10 to 12 minutes or until cookies are crisp.

125

Christmas

Snowball Surprises

8 ounces butter or margarine, softened
¾ cup sugar
1 teaspoon vanilla
2 cups flour, sifted
8 ounces Hershey's Kisses, unwrapped
powdered sugar

Cream the butter or margarine and sugar. Add the vanilla and mix well. Add flour, combine well, and wrap in plastic and refrigerate for half an hour.

Preheat oven to 350°F. Take dough out of refrigerator and break into balls large enough to cover a Hershey's Kiss. Insert the Kiss, making sure it is completely covered. Bake on ungreased cookie sheet until cooked through, about 10 to 12 minutes. While still warm, sift powered sugar on top. Makes 2½ dozen.

Candy Cane Cookies

1¼ cups sugar
1 cup butter or margarine
2 eggs
¼ cup light corn syrup
1 tablespoon vanilla
3 cups flour
½ teaspoon baking soda
½ teaspoon salt
½ teaspoon red food coloring
¼ teaspoon peppermint extract

In a large bowl, beat the sugar and butter or margarine with an electric mixer on medium speed. Add eggs, syrup, and vanilla. With mixer on low, sift in the flour, baking soda, and salt until well blended. Divide dough in half. Add food coloring and peppermint extract to one half. Wrap each in plastic and refrigerate overnight.

Preheat oven to 375°F. On a lightly floured surface, roll with your hands 1 rounded tablespoon plain dough into a 6-inch rope.

Repeat, using 1 teaspoonful red dough. Place ropes side by side and twist together gently to form a candy cane. Pinch the ends tightly and form one end into a hook. Using a spatula, transfer cookie onto ungreased baking sheet. Repeat with remaining dough, placing cookies 2 inches apart.

Bake for 8 minutes, or until lightly browned. Makes 4½ dozen.

127

Greek Kourabiedes

¾ cup butter or margarine
½ cup powdered sugar
1 egg yolk
4 tablespoons milk, or 2 tablespoons milk and
2 tablespoons brandy
½ teaspoon vanilla
1¾ cup flour
¾ cup ground toasted walnuts
½ teaspoon baking powder
¼ teaspoon salt
additional powdered sugar

Christmas

Preheat oven to 325°F. Using an electric mixer on medium speed, beat the butter or margarine and sugar together until creamy. Add egg yolk, milk, and brandy, if using, and vanilla. Beat well. With the mixer on low, add the flour, ground walnuts, baking powder, and salt. Shape dough into 1-inch balls and place 2 inches apart on an ungreased cookie sheet. Bake for 15 minutes or until golden brown. Remove to cooling rack and sift powdered sugar on top. Makes 3 dozen.

Easy Ideas for Cookie Making

- For younger kids with shorter attention spans, bake cookies to be decorated in advance.

- For decorating, have plenty of colored icing (make a paste of powdered sugar and water, adding a tablespoon of water at a time until you reach the desired consistency, then add food coloring, a drop at a time), sugar sprinkles, silver balls, cinnamon hearts, etc. and pour into small bowls.

- Apply icing with fingers, butter knives, or even new paint brushes.

- Baking cookies can be time-consuming. A week or so before Christmas, gather with friends or family members and have a cookie baking party. Then divvy up the cookies for the holidays.

- Wrap some cookies and put them where they'll be found by your letter carrier, package deliverer, or garbage collector. Pass them out to your regular bus or cab drivers.

One at a Time

My family had a wonderful tradition to avoid the "ripping through the presents" Christmas phenomenon. We would all gather at my grandmother's living room in front of her permanent Christmas tree (it was artificial and she kept it up and decorated year round—it saved work, she proclaimed). Starting with the youngest child, each person would pick one present and deliver it to our grandfather. He would then read the tag and the person would deliver the gift to the appropriate recipient. We would all then watch that person open the present before the process would begin again with the second youngest child. And so on until all the presents were opened. It took a long time—hours in fact—but the anticipation (Would this present be for me? When will I get the next one? What is in the big box in the corner?) made the whole thing memorable.

129

Christmas

Lavender Bath Powder

This is a delicious treat that Grandmom or Mom would love to be surprised with.

⅓ cup dried lavender

mortar and pestle

1¼ cups cornstarch

25 drops lavender essential oil

small box and ribbon

With a mortar and pestle, grind the lavender into a fine dust. Mix together with the cornstarch. Stirring constantly, slowly add the essential oil drops and mix well. Place in a beautiful box and tie with a ribbon.

The Day Doesn't Matter

Since most of our children have grown and now have homes of their own, we have started celebrating Christmas at our house on the third Saturday in December. That's the day that we eat, exchange gifts, and gather around the tree for the reading of the Christmas story from Luke. We use this as a special time of worship and prayer.

This gives our older children the chance to stay at their homes or spend time with other relatives at Christmas. Are the rest of us disappointed for making special arrangements for them? No. Christmas is Christmas—any day you make it. On December 25, we now have the joy of serving as volunteers at one of the homeless shelters or at the local Ronald McDonald house.

Dinner at Grandma's

Growing up, I was always proud of and fascinated by my German/Danish grandmother, and the almost unimaginably exotic and arduous life she had led, up to and including her imprisonment in a Nazi work camp near the end of the war for hiding a Jewish friend in her parents' barn. Though my father and his seven brothers and sisters had been flung wide by fate and families, everyone, but *everyone*, showed up at my grandmother's for Christmas dinner. There were always way too many people for anyone to get comfortable, and my grandmother's ancient Pomeranian, Cognac, viciously threatened the fingers of anyone careless or reckless enough to disturb his arthritic slumber, but none of that mattered when the dinner was laid on. The array was awesome in its extent and variety: a turkey and a goose (my sister and I were horrified by the latter after having viewed some now long-forgotten cartoon about a beloved family gosling), three kinds of stuffing, two kinds of cranberry sauce, mashed potatoes, potatoes au gratin, scalloped potatoes, and on and on. Ironically, in

131

Christmas

view of all this bounty, the *piece de resistance* was always my grandmother's stollen, the recipe for which had been passed down many years before from her own eccentric, cigar-smoking grandmother, and was rumored to be absolutely beyond duplication. Not once in all those years did I ever save enough room for that stomach-boggling, weighty treat, but the few bites I managed to squeeze in were always as heavenly as promised. My grandmother would be proud of my religious avoidance and downright disdain of the store-bought variety, which she hardly found even suitable for, as she put it, "stoppering a door!"

Easy Stollen

1 package dry yeast
¼ cup lukewarm water
⅔ cup milk
½ cup butter or margarine
¼ cup sugar
1 egg
½ teaspoon almond extract
½ teaspoon salt
3¼ to 3½ cups sifted all-purpose flour
¾ cup slivered almonds, toasted
1 cup golden raisins
½ cup halved candied cherries
Powdered sugar icing

Preheat oven to 350°F, and grease a baking sheet. Dissolve yeast in water. Scald milk; add butter or margarine and sugar, and stir until sugar is dissolved. Cool to lukewarm. Beat egg and add to milk mixture with yeast, almond extract, and salt. Stir in 2 cups flour and beat until smooth. Stir in almonds, raisins, and cherries. Add remaining flour, and mix until smooth. Cover and let rise in warm place until doubled in bulk, about 1½ hours. Punch down; knead lightly, and pat to 12-inch circle. Fold in half and press edges together firmly. Place on greased baking sheet. Brush top with melted butter. Let rise ½ hour in warm place. Bake for about 30 minutes. Spread top with icing while still warm. Makes 1 large loaf.

133

Christmas

The Spirit of Giving

My parents always taught me that Christmas was a time for giving as well as receiving, and it has become a deeply ingrained habit. When I was growing up, we would always make holiday baskets for the people in our small town we knew were in need—baskets of food and warm socks, and a few toys. Since I have been on my own, I always take $100 (more than I spend on anyone else) and go to a five-and-dime store and buy as many inexpensive, old-fashioned fun presents as I can—balsa-wood airplanes and play dough and jacks and tiddley winks and puzzles and doctor kits—and donate them to Toys for Tots. I get such great pleasure from it; the smell of the store, the toys themselves, bring back such happy childhood memories that even though I don't get to see the look on the kids' faces when they get their gifts, I am completely satisfied.

134

Magical Memories

It was 1924. I was five years old. Overnight, after Thanksgiving, the world had become a fairyland. Snow transformed the city into a white wonder world. Big-wheeled wagons were put away and larger work sleighs pulled by massive horses moved along the frozen streets.

Anticipation infused the air. Santa Claus was coming soon and he would bring me a present. Parental advice not to expect too much because of financial constraints was dismissed. Santa Claus brought presents—you did not have to pay. There was joy and peace and kindness everywhere. People seemed to be trying to outdo Santa in caring for the needy.

My faith was justified. Santa brought me a wonderful mechanical auto, "Leaping Lena." When a spring was wound, the car would run along, suddenly break in the middle like a bucking horse, then reassemble itself and continue on.

Every year since, that same ambience returned after Thanksgiving. Every year, Santa brought me a gift. Five years later, some of my older friends told me there was no Santa Claus. I, of course, knew they were wrong.

Every year, I see the same spirit of kindness and love filling the atmosphere as people reach out to help others in need. Every year, our family gathers around the Christmas tree to see what Santa has brought us. I have never been disappointed. This year, 1997, my wife, children, and grandchildren will gather to share the fruits of Santa's visit. I will be feeling the same sense of anticipation I did in 1924. I will eagerly unwrap my gift to see what Santa brought me. There will always be large children who believe in Santa Claus, who know more than the older, wiser kids. I know, because I am one of them.

135

Christmas

Boxing Day

Laughter can be more satisfying than honor;
more precious than money;
more heart-cleansing than prayer.

—Harriet Rochlin

Community Frivolity

In the United States, the characterless day after Christmas is something of a letdown. Not so in England where it is known as Boxing Day, which has its own particular festivities, more outer-oriented than those at Christmas. This day is about friends, parties, and general frivolity. Its heart is the pantomime, that uniquely British form of entertainment ... but I get ahead of myself.

Traditionally, December 26th was the day local merchants knocked on the doors of the big houses they served (tradesman's entrance, of course) to collect their Christmas boxes or annual tips. Growing up, our house was not only small, but decidedly servantless and though horse-drawn coal and vegetable carts, baker, milkman and fishmonger vans came around the streets, they didn't call on us for gifts. Nevertheless, the upbeat mood of the day lives on, despite the lapse in the old traditions.

As kids, the annual trip to the "panto" fairly pulled the breath out of us. Pantomimes evolved from the medieval traveling mime groups, and play in most theaters for a few weeks around Christmas. Based on a fairy-tale or nursery rhyme (Cinderella, Puss-in-Boots, Red Riding Hood), the story is loosely told by the most improbable actors. Nothing is really what it seems to be. The Principal Boy (Prince or

Hero) is always played by a girl in high heels and tights. The Dame (Old Woman or General Buffoon) is played by a man in drag, usually a well-known comic. The comedy is obvious and raucous, with plenty of slapstick humor and enough double-entendre jokes to keep the adults titillated. The characters strut and preen in overexaggerated camp, and, of course, involve the audience in loudly venting opinions and taking sides. In the end, the hero and heroine unite, the Dame vanquishes all the evil characters, and both cast and audience join in a huge and hilarious sing-a-long.

Once home, and after tea, extended family and friends arrive for the party. Silly games such as Pin the Donkey's Tail and Spin the Platter are enthusiastically played. We kids snicker at Grandpa doing undignified things and being gently scolded by Gramma. The evening ends in another sing-a-long. Mother plays the piano. Dad tootles his Swanee Whistle. Mr. H. scrapes his violin. We kids fashion a kind of kazoo from tissue paper-covered combs that tickle our lips unbearably but don't deter our inept but enthusiastic participation. Pans beaten with wooden spoons complete the band. Christmas carols, old English folk tunes, Gilbert and Sullivan, even some slightly naughty ditties, we sing and play them all with gusto. A laughter-filled, happily exhausting follow-up to Christmas.

139

Boxing Day

The Play's the Thing

For those of us who don't traditionally celebrate Boxing Day, the day after Christmas can, indeed, be quite a letdown, particularly for kids. Why not incorporate a bit of the British sensibility and put on an impromptu play yourselves? Everyone can have fun in the planning during the day and execution at night. Sheets can be costumes, neighbor adults and children can be enlisted as participants and/or audience. Stick with a very simple story, camp it up as the Brits do, and watch the laughter roll.

Easy Supper

Even if you don't celebrate Boxing Day, chances are you won't be up to cooking the day after Christmas. If leftovers don't sound appealing, why not throw together a simple soup and salad dinner? The garlic bread makes it special.

Clam Chowder

To make this without meat, simply use 2 tablespoons of olive oil to sauté the onion.

¼ pound salt pork or bacon, diced
4 medium sized onions, chopped

I cup clam broth (if using canned clams,
the liquid in the can will work)
2 cups diced potatoes
I quart milk
3 cups chopped clams
I teaspoon salt
½ cup flour, mixed well with 2 tablespoons
melted butter
pepper and dried thyme to taste

Brown the salt pork in a large pot or kettle until it is crisp. Add the onions and sauté until light yellow and translucent. Add the clam broth, potatoes, milk, clams, salt, and butter-flour mixture. Cook over medium heat (without boiling) for 15 to 20 minutes, or until potatoes are nicely softened. Add pepper and thyme to taste. Serves 6 to 8.

141

Boxing Day

Garlic Bread

I pound loaf French bread
8 tablespoons butter, softened
3 or 4 garlic cloves, pressed
⅓ cup freshly grated Parmesan cheese
¾ teaspoon dried marjoram or oregano

Preheat oven to 350°F. Cut the loaf into ½ or ¾-inch slices, leaving the bottom crust attached. Cream the butter and garlic together, then add cheese and herbs. Spread each slice liberally with the mixture, then bake, tightly wrapped in aluminum foil, for 15 to 20 minutes.

Kwanzaa

December 26–January 1

*I had a heritage,
rich and nearer than the tongue which gave it voice.
My mind resounded with the words
and my blood raced to the rhythms.*

—Maya Angelou

Tracing the Lineage

Kwanzaa is a Kiswahili word meaning "the first fruits of the harvest." It begins December 26 and lasts for seven days, ending with Karamu, a feast. Kwanzaa was founded in 1966 by Dr. Maulana "Ron" Karenga, a college professor and African American leader who believed that a special holiday could help African Americans meet our goals of building strong families, learning about our history, and creating a sense of unity. In our family, we light the candles every night and then my father reads the names of all those people on both sides of the family that came before us that we know of and we give thanks for all their hard work. Then someone in the family, chosen before, pours water or juice from the unity cup into a bowl. That person then drinks from the cup and raises it high saying *Harambee*, which means "Let's all pull together." All of us repeat *Harambee!* seven times and each person drinks from the cup. Then we all call out the names of African American heroes and we talk about the great things these people did. Then we have dinner, while listening to African music. It creates a wonderful feeling of connection, not only with my family, but with all African Americans, that I look forward to all week.

Family History Book

Here's a Kwanzaa gift that can be passed down from generation to generation.

3-ring hole puncher
50 sheets of 8½-by-11-inch paper
2 8½-by-11-inch pieces of cardboard
length of red, black, or green thin ribbon
hot glue gun
fabric glue
red, green, and black fabric and beads

145

Kwanzaa

Punch all the paper on the left side, making sure all the holes match up when stacked. Do the same with the cardboard. Place one piece of board on top of the paper stack and one board underneath. Put one end of the ribbon into the first hole and the other end of the ribbon into the third hole. String through and bring both ends of the ribbon up through the second hole. Tie and knot the ends together.

Decorate the front and back of the book by gluing fabric and beads to the cardboard. You may want to put your family's name on the cover as well.

Fill the pages with memories of your ancestors and stories from your family. Perhaps you would like to include a family tree in the front. Every year at Kwanzaa, each family member can add a favorite memory from that year.

Creating Family Unity

It's amazing to me that a mere six years ago, we didn't even know about a ceremony that has become a cornerstone of our family life. Now we can't imagine December without Kwanzaa.

When our older son was still a toddler, we started worrying that he might become saturated by the overblown commercialization all around him. To us, the real meaning of Christmas was being lost amid the endless advertising hype and hubbub. Then, my mother-in-law, Jesse, introduced us to a wonderful new tradition, started in the early '60s by an African American man. The first time it felt a little strange because we didn't know much about it, but we've come to love this ceremony.

Now, at midday every December 26, our entire family gathers together to light the *kanara*, a candelabra holding seven candles—three red ones, three green, and one black— representing the seven days of Kwanzaa. The children talk about the parts of their lives they most appreciate, and we all reflect on what family really means, on how fortunate we are. We spend the next six days pondering important principles such as work ethics, responsibility, and self-determination.

We still celebrate Christmas, we still buy a tree and put it in our living room. But we also keep in the living room the *kanara*, stored on a straw mat (called the *mkeka*) with two stalks of dried corn, representing our children. We drink water from a unity cup in honor of our ancestors.

Christmas to us is not about giving presents but about family unity. Kwanzaa has given us stability, a foundation.

Nonmaterial Gifts

Kwanzaa

Those who celebrate Kwanzaa are committed to it remaining as nonmaterialistic as possible. While there is usually a gift component, the gifts are meant to be small and not expensive, hopefully free. Here are eight wonderful gifts in that spirit, found in a newsletter called *Jumpin' Jan's Flash*:

- the gift of listening
- the gift of affection
- the gift of laughter
- the gift of a note of love or appreciation
- the gift of a compliment
- the gift of a favor
- the gift of solitude
- the gift of a cheerful disposition

Dried Rose Heart

This is a lovely homemade present from the heart.

2 dozen dried roses

**2 feet 16-gauge wire (available at
craft or hardware store)**

hot glue gun

7 feet ½-inch wide white or gold ribbon

148

Cut the rosebuds from the stems. Set aside. Take the wire and make a hook at each end. Bend it into a heart shape and hook the ends together at the bottom.

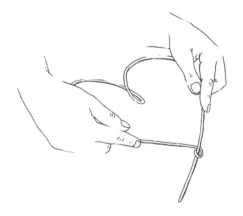

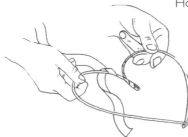

Hot-glue one end of the ribbon to the center of the heart and wrap the ribbon all the way around the heart. When you reach the beginning, hot-glue the ribbon again to the center. With the excess, create a loop by tying the ribbon end to the heart-center.

149

Kwanzaa

With the heart flat on a table, hot glue the rosebuds to the ribbon-covered wire. Hang in closet as a scenter or in room as a decoration.

Around the Table

I love Kwanzaa because it helps me remember what is important in life. It's based on seven principles, which are called *Nguzo Saba*. They are *umoja* (unity), *kujichagulia* (self-determination), *ujima* (collective work and responsibility), *ujamaa* (cooperative economics), *nia* (purpose), *kuumba* (creativity), and *imani* (faith). Each night for seven nights, someone in the family lights the seven candles and does a reading on the principle of the day. Then we talk about what it means. We go around in a circle and speak, so everyone gets a chance to get a word in. My favorite day is always the discussion on *nia*, purpose. It's so easy in the distractions of day-to-day life to forget we are each here to fulfill a special destiny. I like being reminded.

Homemade *Kanara*

If you don't have a *kanara* it's easy to make your own. Simply find a 2-by-4-inch piece of wood (a piece of driftwood would be particularly attractive) and get seven screw-in candle holders (available at most hardware stores). Screw them into the wood and you are ready.

Karamu Feast

Here are some simple recipes that combine African and American flavors, a perfect Kwanzaa combination.

Peanut Butter Soup

Peanuts (also called ground nuts) are a staple of many African tribes.

2 tablespoons oil
4 boneless, skinless chicken breasts,
cut into bite-sized pieces
1 diced onion
1 jalapeño, minced
2 cups water
2 tablespoons peanut butter
1 large tomato, chopped

151

Kwanzaa

Over medium to high heat, heat the oil in a large saucepan and add the chicken, turning until lightly browned. Remove from pan. Add the onions and jalapeño and sauté until limp.

In a small bowl, combine ½ cup of water with the peanut butter until smooth. Add to pan along with remaining water, chicken, and tomato. Bring to a boil, then lower heat and simmer 15 minutes. Serves 4.

Seafood Gumbo

The word *gumbo* comes from the Bantu name for okra— *guingombo*. The secret to good gumbo is to prepare it the day before you want to eat it. It's easy to make, once you get past the chopping.

¼ pound Andouille sausage, sliced
2 tablespoons olive oil
1 cup chopped onions
½ cup chopped red bell pepper
½ cup chopped green bell pepper
½ cup chopped celery
4 cloves garlic, minced
1 14-ounce can cut-up tomatoes
¼ teaspoon Tabasco sauce
salt and pepper, to taste
1 bay leaf
1 cup chicken broth
1 pound large shrimp, cleaned and deveined
1 pound sea scallops
1 package frozen okra

In a large saucepan, sauté the sausage in the oil until lightly browned. Add the onions, peppers, celery, and garlic and sauté until vegetables are limp. Add remaining ingredients, except the seafood and okra, and bring to a boil. Lower the heat and simmer covered for 10 minutes. Add the seafood and okra and return to a boil and cook until seafood is cooked through, about 5 minutes. Remove the bay leaf and serve over rice. Serves 4.

Great Greens

3 cups water
1 smoked ham hock
1½ pound assorted greens (mustard, collard, beet,
turnip), washed, stemmed, and chopped
½ teaspoon molasses
salt and pepper to taste

In a medium saucepan, bring water and ham hock to a boil. Cover, reduce heat to low, and simmer for 1½ hours. Remove hock and allow to cool slightly, then remove meat from the bone. Discard bone, add meat back to pot, and add remaining ingredients. On medium heat, cook, stirring frequently, until greens are tender, about 15 minutes. Serves 4.

153

Kwanzaa

Sweet Potato Pie

2 cups sweet potatoes, cooked
4 tablespoons butter or margarine
3 eggs
1 cup sugar
1 teaspoon cinnamon
¼ teaspoon grated nutmeg
¾ cup milk
1 teaspoon vanilla
1 9-inch pie shell, baked
¼ cup chopped pecans, optional

Preheat oven to 375°F. Mash sweet potatoes together with melted butter or margarine in a large bowl. Blend in eggs, sugar, cinnamon, nutmeg, milk, and vanilla and mix well. Pour mixture into baked pie shell and bake in the oven for about 35 to 45 minutes or until it doesn't jiggle. When there is about 5 minutes cooking time left, sprinkle on pecans if using. Serves 8.

154

Herbal Soap Balls

Here's an easy, inexpensive homemade gift that the little ones can help with. The kids will love the pulverizing, and recipients will like its clean fragrance.

I tablespoon pulverized dried herbs, pulverized (you can use rosemary, sage, thyme, or peppermint, or a combination)
5 drops matching essential oil
I personal size Ivory soap bar, shredded and placed in a mixing bowl

Pour ¼ cup boiling water over the herbs and add the essential oil. Let steep for 20 minutes. Bring this mixture to a boil and pour over the soap. When cool enough, mix well by hand and let stand 15 minutes. Mix again and form into three balls. Place on plastic wrap and let stand 3 days. Makes 3 soap balls.

New Year's Eve

December 31

Ring out, wild bells, to the wild sky,
The flying cloud, the frosty light:
The year is dying in the night;
Ring out, wild bells, and let him die.

Ring out the old, ring in the new,
Ring, happy bells, across the snow:
The year is going, let him go;
Ring out the false, ring in the true.

—Alfred Lord Tennyson,
from "Ring Out Wild Bells"

Adult Sleepover

My favorite New Year's Eve is celebrated with friends via a small potluck dinner and slumber party (no worrying about driving home). We eat, tell stories, play games, and drink a little champagne before going to sleep. On New Year's morning, when we awake to the smell of coffee and bagels, I am thankful to be alive. Not only is the holiday eating, drinking, and gift-giving over, but I feel fortunate to start the year with a morning walk in the company of friends.

Eighteen-Carat Eggnog

Only you can decide if drinking this glorious eggnog during the holiday season is worth the risk of consuming raw eggs. The recipe's creator has been making it for years with no ill effects—she claims the alcohol kills any bacteria. She also says the longer it ages, the better it tastes, and it will keep refrigerated for up to a year.

9 egg yolks
2½ cups superfine sugar
3⅓ cups (1 750-ml bottle) bourbon
1½ cups plus 2 tablespoons light rum

1½ cups plus 2 tablespoons brandy
1 quart heavy cream
2 cups half-and-half
freshly grated nutmeg

Whisk the yolks and the sugar together by hand in a large bowl (a 13-quart one works best). Slowly stir in the bourbon, rum, brandy, cream, and half-and-half. Pour into glass jars and refrigerate, covered for *at least* three days. Shake it up *very well* before serving. Serve over ice with a sprinkle of freshly grated nutmeg. Sip slowly and enjoy! Serves 12.

157

New Year's Eve

A Magical Moment

I was about eight and my brother was about ten. We were at our father's and stepmother's house for New Year's Eve. They were having a party and we were supposed to be in bed. But we were wide awake and so we concocted a plan. We snuck downstairs and took a bunch of streamers from the tables and cut some into confetti. Around midnight, we snuck out of bed and hid ourselves so that we could see over the balcony into the living room. It was dark; the only light was the flickering of the fire and the candles around the room. It was exciting to be spying on adults. As they began the countdown to midnight, my brother and I began to throw streamers and confetti over the railing onto the adults below. It was a magical moment, for us and for them.

A Jar of Good Fortune

If I am invited to someone's house for a New Year's Eve party, I always bring a jar of fortune cookies as a gift. People love opening them and seeing what their message for the new year is.

Playing Fun

My group of friends always holds a board game tournament for New Year's Eve. We arrive early, around 5 P.M., game boards in hand, have a potluck supper, and then commence playing. The more the merrier, because then there can be a game of Risk going on in one room, while Pictionary is being played in another, and Dictionary in yet another. People decide what they want to play and as their game finishes, roam around looking to join another group or start a new game. It all goes on until the wee hours of the morning.

Gastronomic Travel

Since my daughter was about five (she is now ten), we have "traveled" to a different country each New Year's Eve via dinner. We look for recipes that have familiar ingredients and those I can enlist her help on. Our favorite has been Italy. We have made gnocchi twice in the last five years on New Year's Eve. We have also traveled to India, Mexico, Switzerland, and China. It's only October, and my daughter is asking which country we are going to for this New Year's Eve.

159

New Year's Eve

Don't Rain on My Parade

New Year's always brings back memories of childhood in Los Angeles. When I was in junior high school, my family would pack up an overnight camping kit and head to Pasadena to spend New Year's Eve on the Tournament of Roses Parade route. In order to claim a good spot, we had to leave around noon; arriving an hour later, we'd find a place to park and then decide where to lay out the blankets to start the all-day-and-night task of protecting our territory. We were never alone; many other people began camping days before.

Our family liked to claim a spot near the beginning of the parade. The marchers were fresh, the flowers on the float had not been shaken off yet, and sometimes the parade would begin and then stop and we would get a long look at the participants. One year, Kate Smith was the Grand Marshall and the parade stopped with her in front of us. After a bit, she started to sing "God Bless America" and everyone around us sang along. One year, Stanford University made it to the Rose Bowl, and as you might suspect, when their band marched by, it was the only band that was not in neat columns and rows. At least they played great music.

When the weather permitted, we'd while away the hours playing Monopoly, Parcheesi, Yahtzee, and my favorite, Risk, until 3:00 or 4:00 in the morning. Often we would invite the folks camped next to us to join in. Most people we met were only friends for the day, but a few have stayed friends to this day. I'm starting a family and plan to carry on the tradition with my children.

Family Time

I have never been a big New Year's Eve party girl—it's too hard for me to stay up late, and loud, drunken parties were never my scene anyway. Since my kids have gotten school age, we have instituted a New Year's Eve tradition that everyone loves. We have dinner at a normal time and then we turn out all the lights, gather on pillows in front of the fire, and light a special family candle. We take turns talking about the past year—what we remember that was particularly good, things that were hard, and what lessons we learned. Then we each say what we are going to work on or contemplate for the next year and together, we blow out the candle. Because we only do this once a year, it has a special quality; even the older kids willingly participate.

161

New Year's Eve

Love Pledges

This New Year's Eve, instead of New Year's resolutions, why not have each member of your family take a pledge to make some kind of new year change in their life on behalf of those they love? Be sure to make it both concrete *and* realistic: Rather than saying, "I promise never to smoke again," how about, "I know that smoking is bad for me and it hurts you to see me smoke. Because you care about me, I promise to take the SmokeEnders class in February and try my best to stick with it." People can work on any negative habit—

biting fingernails, workaholism, spendthriftiness, etc. Just be sure to make it a goal that is reachable—not, "I'll never work late again," but "at least two nights a week I pledge to try to be home before the kids are in bed." And if you do this, be sure everyone understands that what people are pledging to is to *try.* We are all imperfect and fallible. Impossible standards just lead to lying and sneaking around.

162

Celebration for Two

To me, New Year's Eve is grown-up time. I always put the kids to bed early and then make my husband a candlelight dinner. It is always the same menu, based on my French heritage: escargot in garlic butter, cheese soufflé, a green salad made with butter lettuce garnished with thinly sliced onions and dressed with white vinegar, sugar, salt, and pepper (Really! It's great. You don't miss the oil at all.), and finally, crème brûlée. We sit quietly by the fire, have our romantic meal around 10:00 P.M., stare into one another's eyes, and contemplate our lives together. Truly memorable!

Cheese Soufflé

butter or margarine for the dish
1¼ cups milk (may be low-fat)
1 bay leaf
3 tablespoons butter
3 tablespoons flour
4 egg yolks
salt and pepper to taste
2 teaspoons Dijon mustard
1 cup grated sharp cheddar cheese
6 egg whites

Preheat the oven to 375° F. Butter well a six-cup soufflé pan, including the sides of the pan.

In a small saucepan, heat the milk with the bay leaf until it comes to a boil. Set aside.

In a medium saucepan, melt the butter over low heat. Add the flour and whisk well, cooking for several minutes. Remove the bay leaf from the milk and whisk milk into the flour mixture. Stir until mixture thickens, about 5 minutes. Remove from heat, add the egg yolks one at a time, the salt and pepper, and the mustard. Stir in the cheese.

In a glass bowl, whip the egg whites with a pinch of salt until they form stiff peaks. Add a bit of whites to the yolk mixture, then fold the remaining whites gently in. Pour carefully into soufflé pan and bake until golden brown on top and firm in the center, about 30 minutes. Serves 4.

163

New Year's Eve

Quick Crème Brûlée

This is incredibly easy. I make a lot so we can have it all week.

4 cups heavy cream
I vanilla bean, split in half lengthwise
7 egg yolks
½ cup plus 1½ tablespoons sugar for the custard plus
7 teaspoons sugar for topping

164

Preheat oven to 350°F. In a large saucepan over high heat, combine the cream and vanilla bean and bring to a boil, stirring occasionally with a wire whisk to prevent sticking.

Meanwhile, in a mixing bowl, whisk together egg yolks and the ½ cup plus 1½ tablespoons sugar until well blended. As soon as the cream boils, immediately pour it in a slow, steady stream into the egg-sugar mixture, whisking constantly.

Strain the cream-egg mixture through a fine-mesh sieve into 7 ramekins, each 3½ inches in diameter and 2¼ tall, dividing it evenly. Place the ramekins in a shallow baking pan and pour in hot water to reach halfway up the sides of the ramekins. Bake until the custard is firm to the touch, about 1 hour and 10 minutes. Remove from the oven and remove the ramekins from the baking pan. Let cool completely, then cover and refrigerate until well chilled, 2-3 hours.

Preheat the broiler. Sprinkle 1 teaspoon of the sugar evenly over the top of each chilled ramekin. Place them on a baking sheet. Place the sheet in the broiler about 4 inches from the heat source and broil until the sugar caramelizes, about 5 minutes. Remove from the broiler and serve immediately. Serves 7.

Remembering Hogmanay

I go back a few years to the times when my dear husband, Alex, seriously enacted some ancient Scottish rites—in the north of England, yet. Of course, he was a Scot (never say Scotch, which is a drink), but many Scottish customs had filtered virtually intact, over the border. Ask a Scot to name the year's most important holiday and invariably, face aglow, he'll answer, "Hogmanay." That's New Year's Eve to us. It was then more important than Christmas, when some folks didn't even get the day off. In contrast, Hogmanay revels were elaborate and had an intensity about them unrivaled anywhere. The heart of the all-night celebration lay in the strange ritual of "first-footing." It would begin as the last strains of "Auld Lang Syne" faded. Custom (or superstition) has it that to bring maximum good fortune to a household for the New Year, the first foot to strike over the threshold after midnight must belong to a handsome dark-haired man who is not a family member. He must also bring a specific collection of symbolic gifts for the house.

165

New Year's Eve

Alex, being dark-haired and modestly handsome, immersed himself in this ritual. Being the genuine article, he is much in demand with many houses to "first-foot." The details of the ritual are serious and precise. He took it on every year with a mix of humor and solemnity. The day before, he pulled out his kilt and full regalia. It had to be in tip-top shape for its annual outing. Each household was be presented with four gifts: a tiny bag of salt to symbolize good health; a miniature log or piece of coal to be thrown on the fire to ensure warmth throughout the year; some shortbread or fruitcake to bring ample food; and most importantly, the "wee dram" of whiskey which makes certain the household will always have an ample supply of that vital Scottish brew. Each gift has to be tied up in a festive ribbon. This, Alex did laboriously and meticulously with stiff, unaccustomed fingers. The bundles, finally ready, were packed into baskets, along with our more formal New Year's presents.

After midnight, braving whatever the elements would bring, we set off, noisily greeting other groups with a similar mission. The hilarity gradually increased as at each house we were welcomed ceremoniously and Alex stepped over the threshold to laughter, cheers, and kisses. The gifts were presented and in return we were regaled with ample refreshments.

About four in the morning, Alex's duties were done, some eight or ten households assured of a prosperous New Year. We trudged wearily, and a little unsteadily, homeward to "first-foot" our own house. Alex had freezing cold knees, but tradition was respected.

New Year's Eve

New Year's Day

January 1

You do too much.
Go and do nothing for a while.
Nothing.

—Lillian Hellman

Doing Nothing

I love New Year's Day because it is the one day of the year that I do absolutely nothing. It feels so good after all the rushing around of the holiday season. I stay in bed as long as I can, reading the novel I've been wanting to get to all year, but never had time for. Sometimes I forage out to the refrigerator and bring back cheddar cheese, crackers, and pickles to my bed. If the weather is good, I might venture out in the afternoon for a quiet walk. In the evening, after another scavenged meal, I sit by the fire and finish up my book. It's wonderful because it feels so self-indulgent. If the holiday falls on a Saturday, I do the same on Sunday as well. Then it's doubly delicious.

Soda Bread

This sweet, crumbly loaf is delicious for breakfast. You can make it a day or two before so all you have to do on New Year's Day is wake up and enjoy.

4 cups flour
1 teaspoon salt
1 teaspoon baking soda
1 cup sugar

¾ cup butter
1 cup currants or raisins
1½ cups buttermilk

Preheat oven to 350°F, and grease a cookie sheet. Sift the dry ingredients together in a large bowl. Add the butter with a pastry blender or a fork until well combined. Add the raisins and then gradually add the buttermilk. Turn dough onto a floured board and knead for one minute, adding more flour if necessary to knead (mixture should be quite sticky).

Divide the dough in two and form into balls. Place on cookie sheet and, with a knife, carve a cross or an X on the top. Brush top with buttermilk and bake until golden brown, about 40 minutes. Makes 2 loaves.

New Year's Day

Easy Ideas for Making
New Year's Day Meaningful

- Consider creating a ritual summing-up of the past year. One very simple thing to do is to write on a piece of paper what you want to let go of and burn it in the fireplace or over the stove. Then write on another piece of paper what you want to take hold of and put it in a safe place.

- Create a question for the year and consult some divination tool—runes, tarot cards, feng shui cards, animal wisdom cards, etc.—and write down what it says.

- Gather family members and talk about what you learned this past year. Choose a quality you all want to work on and dedicate the coming year to that quality, for example, 1999 is the Year of Compassion. Or each of you select your own quality or virtue to work on individually.

- Find a friend or family member who is interested in making the same resolution as you (more exercise, daily journal writing, whatever) and agree to support one another in working on it.

- Contemplate how the spirit moves in your life. From what unexpected areas has it come into your life? How has it changed you? What is it calling you to do now? Perhaps this is something your family can discuss together at dinner.

- Use this day to mend a fence, get over a grudge, forgive someone, reach out to someone who is in pain.

- We are not just here to take up space, but to serve. Are you using your unique talents and gifts on behalf of the larger whole? How can you begin to allow yourself to contribute to the world? What new actions are you being called toward?

Nature's Hangover Cure

If you have imbibed a bit too much on New Year's Eve, you might want to give the following a try:

1 tablespoon finely chopped fresh ginger root
1 teaspoon grated lemon peel
2 cups water
¼ cup culinary rose water
1 drop peppermint oil

Combine the ginger root, lemon peel, and water in a covered pot and bring to a boil. Simmer ten minutes. Strain out ginger and lemon peel pieces and cool the remaining liquid. Add rose water and oil of peppermint. Drink ½ cup at room temperature every two hours, along with plenty of water.

New Year's Day

Hoppin' John

It's said in the South that if you eat Hoppin' John on New Year's Day, you will have good luck all year. No one knows exactly where the recipe originated, but certain West African dishes are somewhat similar, as is the Peas and Rice of the Caribbean. Where the name comes from is also shrouded in mystery. To make this vegetarian, simply omit the ham hocks and add a bit of soy sauce.

1½ cups dry black-eyed peas
4 cups water
1½ cups chopped onions
3 cloves garlic, chopped
½ teaspoon pepper

¼ teaspoon red pepper
1 bay leaf
8 ounces ham hocks
salt and pepper

Bring peas and water to a boil in a large saucepan. Boil two minutes and remove from heat. Let stand 1 hour. Add remaining ingredients, cover and simmer for two hours, stirring frequently. Add more water if necessary. Remove ham hocks and bay leaf, add salt and pepper to taste. Serve over rice. Serves 4.

174

A New Year's Soak

I love to take a long, luxurious bath first thing on January 1. It's a great antidote to all the partying, late nights, food, and drink of the past few weeks. I use a tub tea sachet (Cozy Weather is my favorite), and just lie there, adding more hot water as it cools too much. I think about the past year, the highlights and the lowlights, and I contemplate what my hopes and dreams are for the coming year. It's my personal renewal ritual.

Aromatic Indulgences

Aromatherapy, the use of scents to enhance mood and health, has been gaining in popularity in recent years. And what better time to indulge than after the holidays, when mind and body could really use some rejuvenation. For relaxing in the new year, consider the following aromatherapy bath, courtesy of the Aroma Therapeutix catalog (800-308-6284). Other good sources of tub teas, bubble baths, essential oils, and other sensual self-care products are Earthsake stores (510-848-5023), Bare Escentuals catalog and stores (800-227-3990), Body Time catalog and stores (510-524-0360), The Body Shop catalog and stores (800-541-2535), Green World Mercantile (415-771-5717), Red Rose catalog and stores (800-374-5505), Hearthsong catalog and stores (800-432-6314), as well as Cost Plus stores.

175

New Year's Day

Frayed Nerves Bath

7 drops lavender essential oil
2 drops sweet marjoram essential oil
3 drops ylang ylang essential oil

Fill tub with warm water and then add oils. Swish around with to evenly disperse and then submerge yourself.

Football Fun

I've never been much of a sports enthusiast, but I never miss the New Year's Bowl games. My husband is a dyed-in-the-wool fan (any team, any time), so we rise early on game day to begin our preparations for the main event. Essential, of course, are ample food and beverage supplies, and the simpler the better: chips and onion dip, Ritz crackers and supermarket cheese, pretzels, pork rinds, and peanuts, not to mention plenty of canned (domestic only, of course) beer and soda, on plenty of ice. Then we're ready to welcome a bevy of friends and football fans (every team affiliation welcome—the better for rival cheering sections). Then the games begin, and it's American *über*-spectacle at its finest; the fans, the teams, the cheerleaders. There's something exciting and, dare I say, inspiring, about connecting with millions of fellow Americans in support of what is essentially the world's largest game of catch. I never manage to stick with the games play-by-play (and is it just me, or does it get longer every year?) but I never switch the set off after the games without feeling just a little more American!

New Year's Potpourri

This is a great use for Christmas tree needles. The recipe is adapted from Gingham and Spice in Gardenville, Pennsylvania.

1 quart dried pine needles

2 cups dried roses

1 cup chopped patchouli leaves

½ cup broken cinnamon sticks

½ cup dried orange peel

1½ teaspoons cedar or pine essential oil

1 tablespoon each allspice, cinnamon, cloves, coriander, mace, and orris root, mixed

handful dried cranberries

handful small pine cones

177

New Year's Day

Combine all ingredients in a potpourri jar and set out.

Open House

Every New Year's afternoon, we host an open house for the entire neighborhood from 3:00 to 5:00 P.M. It started when we first moved into town and didn't know anyone. We just printed up invitations on our computer, making it clear we were inviting the whole neighborhood, and stuck them under the front doors of the houses in the surrounding neigh-borhood. We got quite a turnout—most people work and don't know one another and were eager to meet. Once we got started, everyone wanted to do it again.

It's a very-low key affair—I serve a few simple appetizers and hot mulled cider, and most folks bring something to add to the buffet table. It's a nice way to end the holiday season, and at least we all get a chance to catch up with one another once a year.

Chinese New Year

Corresponds to lunar calendar—around the end of January and beginning of February

Then sing, young hearts that are full of cheer,
With never a thought of sorrow;
The old goes out, but the glad young year
Comes merrily in tomorrow.

—Emily Miller

A Proper Preparation

My grandmother always took the New Year preparations very seriously. In the weeks before, she would thoroughly scrub her apartment from top to bottom (that always involved me with a feather duster, carefully cleaning her intricate statuary that was displayed on a hutch in the living room; until I was about twelve, I thought it was the greatest treat); make sure the family settled any old debts (considered very unlucky to bring into the New Year); adorn the family altar with oranges to bring wealth, tangerines to bring good fortune, and apples for peace; and prepare special "good luck" foods. When I was little, I never knew why we ate certain food; later I learned it was because certain words brought good luck: for example, *san choy* (lettuce) sounded like the word for prosperity; the tones of *ho yau* (oyster sauce) sounded like "good moments." Other foods were considered lucky in and of themselves: candy brought sweetness; steamed buns, good luck and good fortune; melon, growth and good health; coconut brought friendship; pork, wealth. I loved the celebrations because my grandmother was happy then. I spent all my spare time outside school helping her get ready. Those peaceful moments with just the two of us cleaning and cooking will live with me always.

Braised Ginger Pork

According to Chinese tradition, food is the bridge between humans and the gods, "the vehicle," as Deborah Kesten writes in *Feeding the Body, Nourishing the Soul*, "whereby loving intentions and actions can be communicated to the gods and, in turn, reflected back to the people via good fortune."

2 pounds 1-inch pork cubes
a little flour
3 tablespoons peanut oil
⅓ cup chicken broth
⅓ cup soy sauce
2 tablespoons sherry
¼ cup chopped green or yellow onion
1 small clove garlic, crushed or minced
1 tablespoons sugar
1 teaspoon ground ginger
dash pepper
hot, cooked rice

181

Chinese New Year

Dredge meat in flour. Heat peanut oil in Dutch oven or large skillet. Add half of meat and brown quickly; remove meat and set aside. Brown remaining meat; remove and set aside. Pour off excess oil from pan. Combine chicken broth, soy sauce, and sherry. Add onion, garlic, sugar, ginger, and pepper. Place in cooking pan along with meat. Simmer, covered, for 15 minutes, or until meat is tender. Serve over rice. Makes about 6 servings.

A Great Surprise

It was 1920. I was a recent immigrant from Hong Kong and working as a laundry helper in Los Angeles. Poor doesn't begin to describe my situation. On New Year's I joined the parade as a lion dancer, one of the line prancing down the streets of Chinatown, snapping at the heads of lettuce filled with money that hung in front of each store. I got a lucky hit—the lettuce split open and there was a ten-dollar bill. More money than I had seen ever before at one time. I treated all my friends to quite a feast that night!

Explosions of Sounds and Color

As a child growing up in San Francisco, I got a lot of exposure to various cultures and traditions, but it was mainly as an eager, but distant, observer. In the fourth grade, however, I was invited by a Chinese friend and her family to experience the celebration of the New Year in the city's legendary Chinatown. I followed Mei Mei (the diminutive means "little sister" in Mandarin) up a long flight of narrow stairs to her family's apartment above an Asian grocery store on Grant Street, in the heart of Chinatown. For the celebration, Mei's grandmother, her wrinkled apple-doll face split by a wide welcoming smile, had made almond cookies. They were warm and chewy, just out of the oven, each one dotted with a bit of red food coloring (for good luck).

The street was rapidly filling with rapt and excited onlookers, united with the parade's participants in the frenetic celebration of light and noise, as we hurried back down the stairs, armed with heads of lettuce with which to "feed" the fantastic Chinese dragon (ensuring that he will have the strength to chase off evil spirits). We pushed forward through the thronging crowd to perch on the curb for the main event: the dazzling, intricate dance of the parade dragon. The street itself was a feast for the senses—fireworks filled the street with bits of red paper and the pungent odor of gunpowder and smoke, their frenetic crackling cacophony a sharp counterpoint to the ceremonial drums pounded to guide the footsteps of the plumed and sequined dragon. The excitement did not end even after the beast's many legs (two of which belonged to Mei's brother Wendell) had capered past us, for there were many other sights and sounds to experience at the celebration: crispy fried dumplings and sugary candied fruits, brightly colored paper fans and lit paper lanterns. Now that I have a daughter of my own, we make a point of attending the Chinese New Year festivities, which have never lost their magic of pure and extravagant spectacle for me. I

183

Chinese New Year

have always enjoyed traditional Western celebrations of the changing annum, but they lack the unbridled exuberance of that fantastic celebration.

Chinese Almond Cookies

½ cup whole roasted almonds
1 cup sifted all-purpose flour
½ teaspoon baking powder
¼ teaspoon salt
½ cup butter or margarine
⅓ cup granulated sugar
½ teaspoon almond extract
1 tablespoon gin, vodka, or water

Preheat oven to 350°F, and grease several cookie sheets. Reserve 36 whole almonds; finely chop or grind remainder. Sift flour with baking powder and salt. Thoroughly cream butter and sugar in a large bowl. Stir in all remaining ingredients except whole almonds. Form dough into 36 balls. Place on greased cookie sheets. Press a whole almond in the center of each ball, or dot with a bit of red food coloring. Bake for 20 minutes or until lightly browned. Makes about 3 dozen.

Greeting the Gods

Chinese people believe there is a god for every aspect of our lives . . . along with the Kitchen God, there is a god who guards the entrance to your door; a god who takes care of business; a righteousness god; a longevity god....

There's a god for just about everything. He or she comes to inspect you every now and then on his or her own schedule. However, on the eve of Chinese New Year, all of them come. It's of paramount importance to welcome the hierarchy of gods with the best you have.

Grandma scrutinizes every corner of the house, especially the altars. Much as we think they are spotless, she unfailingly discovers tainted spots. Each member of the family is bathed and washed and wearing new clothes. Everyone is excited. After all, the gods, the inspectors, are coming.

This is the most important evening of the year, because if you did anything bad during the last year, this is your chance to receive the blessings of the gods and great fortune for the coming year . . . this is the time when the gods are easily pleased and can't deny your wishes.

185

Chinese New Year

Ringing in the New Year

From the time I was very little, my favorite part of *Yuan Tan* is the sending of the Kitchen God to heaven. My brothers and I would stockpile a good-sized collection of firecrackers. At night, we'd carry the wooden statue of the Kitchen God outside, and set off our firecrackers around its feet. It would catch fire—very dramatic—and go off to make its report to the Emperor of Heaven on how we'd been behaving over the past year. The noise, the flames, the anticipation of its report (which I understood when I was little to be kind of like Santa's naughty or nice)—I look forward to it every year.

Easy Ideas for Celebrating Chinese New Year

- Plant narcissus bulbs in pots about six to eight weeks in advance. If they bloom for Chinese New Year, you will have a prosperous year.

- It is considered very auspicious to give at this time of year. Consider an anonymous act of kindness to a homeless person or a donation to a charity of your choice. Better yet, volunteer some time.

- Use this time of year to do a thorough cleaning of your kitchen—Chinese New Year is the time to start with everything clean and new.

- Hang red banners on which you've written your wishes for the coming year.

- Fill red envelopes with gold foil chocolate coins to give to friends and family.

- Avoid anger during the two-week period—it is considered bad luck. (Traditionally, knives, scissors, and other sharp objects are avoided because they could cut bonds.)

- Invite friends to come over for a midnight supper. In many Chinese traditions, a vegetarian New Year's meal is served at midnight because it is believed that the gods (who don't eat meat) descend at 11:30 P.M. to see how the family has behaved and then must be fed a magnificent feast so they will guard you well in the coming year.

- Consider what blessings you would like to ask for. This is the time when the gods smile kindly on requests.

187

Chinese New Year

'Id al-Fitr

Cycles through the year: the first day of the Muslim month of Shawwal. In upcoming years it will be celebrated in January.

I have learned silence from the talkative,
tolerance from the intolerant, and kindness from the unkind;
yet strange, I am ungrateful to these teachers.

—Kahlil Gibran

Family Fun

'Id al-Fitr, the second most important Islamic holiday, marks the end of the one-month fast of Ramadan and the beginning of a three-day fest. It's a day of great celebrations, prayers, and thanksgiving.

The memories of my childhood in India come back as if it was just yesterday. As a kid—with all my sisters and brothers—we each tried to be the first one to see the new moon, praying for a clear sky. On the expected day, people would be glued to the radios during the evening news hour to find out whether the moon had been sighted or not. If not, it would be declared that 'Id would be the following day. How disappointing for us kids—to wait one more day for all the excitement, new clothes, good food, friends ...! On some cloudy days, the crazy clergymen would get into an argument about the sighting of the new moon—so the 'Id celebrations would get postponed for a day—I hated the *mullahs* for that!

New dresses were ready, ironed, and laid out with new sandals, and, of course, new brightly colored glass bangles and trinkets to match. Who could wait? The house would be immersed in heavenly aroma of my mother's cooking of *Sewaian*—a sweet dish made of hair-thin vermicelli, with nuts, raisins, and saffron, beautifully decorated with *Tabak*—paper-thin silver sheets. An irresistible sight.

But one had to be patient to enjoy all this. With other male members of the family, my father dressed up in his well-pressed, high-collar, black, knee-length coat and light-fitting white pants and a matching black cap to go to the mosque for the special morning prayers. It was interesting for me to see my father going to the mosque—he was not a very religious person, seldom said his prayers, yet he never, ever missed his *'Id namaz* ('Id prayers). This day must have been very special for him. He always looked great in this outfit which was only worn on very special occasions.

By the time the men returned, my mother, sisters, and I would be ready, all dressed up in our beautiful new dresses, juggling the colorful glass bangles in front of the beautifully laid-out big dining table, with loads of sweet-dishes.

A seemingly neverending stream of visitors, friends, and relatives would begin to arrive. We girls would get busy exchanging notes on each others' dresses and how beautiful each one looked. The boys would get busy among them-selves—as a kid I never could understand what they dis-cussed, what they liked; their's was a different world which I never bothered to get to know.

By evening, everyone would be exhausted, yet it would be our turn to call on our family and friends—as many as one could manage. And so would the day end, the day for which we kids would have to wait another whole year to come again!

191

'Id al-Fitr

Gulab Jamun

One of my favorite Indian desserts are these easy-to-make rose-flavored berries.

Syrup:

1 cup sugar
1 cup water
2 teaspoons rosewater or 1 teaspoon rose essence (optional)
½ teaspoon ground cardamom (optional)

Dough:

1 cup whole fat milk powder
2 tablespoons white flour
1½ level teaspoon baking powder
about 8 tablespoons of water
about 8 tablespoons of oil

Make the syrup by mixing the sugar, water, cardamom, and rose water, if using, in a heavy saucepan and bring to a slow boil.

To make the gulabs, mix the dry ingredients in a bowl. Add water a little at a time to make a dough that kneads well. Let sit for 10 minutes. Knead again and form into balls the size of table tennis balls. In a nonstick pan or wok, heat the oil over low heat. Fry the balls until golden brown, turning frequently. Remove from pan with a slotted spoon and drop into steaming hot sugar-syrup. Enjoy warm or cold. Makes 20 Gulab Jamuns.

Endless Delight

When I was growing up in Iraq, 'Id was always eagerly anticipated by all the kids in the village. The holiday began when
we heard the boom of a cannon or the beating of drums.
Beforehand, my mother would have made my sister and I
new silk dresses in bright colors. All dressed up, we would
run to the square where there would be a fair set up with
swings, merry-go-rounds, and a ferris wheel, as well as
roasted chestnut and peanut vendors and even a puppet
show.

The first night, when we went home for dinner at sunset,
we would have Kibbeh and Baklava. The second night was
our favorite, because that's when we would get our presents.
On the third evening, we would visit with all our relatives.
The whole family would be in a happy mood—it was always
the best holiday!

193

'Id al-Fitr

The Joy of Kibbeh

There are as many Kibbeh recipes as there are homes in the
Middle East—Paula Wolfert, in her book *The Cooking of the
Eastern Mediterranean*, calls it the masterpiece of the Middle

Eastern table and offers fifty varieties. Basically it is a bulgur wheat and meat shell that can be stuffed with just about anything. It takes some dexterity to create the shell, so the recipe I have chosen does not require forming a shell or stuffing. This is a Syrian stew, adapted from Wolfert's book. Bulgur is available at health food stores.

Kibbeh Onion and Tomato Stew

For the Kibbeh

⅓ cup bulgur
¼ small onion
¼ pound ground lamb
pinch of ground cumin and paprika
salt

For the stew

2 onions, thinly sliced
2 tablespoons olive oil
1 14½ ounce can tomatoes,
pureed in food processor
salt and pepper to taste
pinch red pepper flakes
pinch of sugar
4 tablespoons chopped fresh parsley

Make the Kibbeh first. Preheat the oven to 450°F. Wash the bulgur in a sieve under running water and allow to drain. Place the onion in the food processor and puree. Add the lamb and seasonings and process until smooth. Add the bulgur and process again for a moment. Knead this "dough" on a flat surface until smooth and pliable. Wet your hands in a bowl of ice water and pinch off bite-sized pieces of the mixture and place on cookie sheet. Repeat until all Kibbeh is used. Bake 3-4 minutes per side, or until brown.

In a frying pan with a lid, combine the sliced onions, olive oil, and enough water to cover the onions. Cover and steam over medium heat for 15 minutes. Add the tomatoes and ½ cup water. Cover and cook for 10 minutes. Add the Kibbeh pieces, the salt and pepper, red pepper, and sugar, and cook, covered for 5 minutes. Add the parsley. Serves 4.

195

'Id al-Fitr

Kids' and Adults' Birthdays

The only gift is a portion of thyself.

—Ralph Waldo Emerson

A Higher Purpose

When I was a child, my father would always say a prayer before dinner on my birthday: "With thanksgiving and love that you have been given to be a part of our hearts and of our family, we celebrate this day of your birth, beautiful child, delightful spirit. May you have a year full of joy and may your prodigious talents, like arrows, find their true mark through a long life in this world."

198

In the presence of these consecrating words, my life became more than simply the life I was leading. It became a holy place, with qualities and possibilities. It became a privilege and a responsibility. No matter what difficult times I came to, no matter what hardships I faced, the ritual of these consecrated words was a beautiful reference that pointed me to my higher purpose.

An Old-Fashioned Taffy Pull

My mother is one of those hardy New Englanders who believes in thriftiness, simplicity, and tradition. So when we were growing up, we always created handmade birthday cards (why buy them when you can make them?) and got books from the library (why buy them when you can borrow them?). She was the mother who taught all the kids in the neighborhood how to make snowmen, and organized the annual neighborhood Christmas carol sing and croquet tournament; if it was about having fun for free (or almost), she was in charge. So of course the taffy pull for my birthday was her idea. We jaded, late twentieth-century kids were skeptical, to say the least—wasn't taffy that horrible colored saltwater stuff sold at beaches along the eastern seaboard, and didn't making the stuff at home go out with high-topped shoes? "Oh pish," she said, "stop being party-poopers" as she rounded up at least seven kids from down the street. "We're going to do it."

And do it we did—and yes it was fun, particularly with a crowd. Now that I am a parent and those values of my mother's seem to be right in vogue, I, too, encourage my kids to make their own cards, and they—and all their friends—love to make taffy together. It's a lot of fun—all you need is a candy thermometer and some pairs of willing arms. But before you start, be sure to read the directions all the way through—it does require some expertise. And above all, don't leave the little ones alone—the hot syrup can be dangerous!

Birthdays

Vanilla Taffy

1¼ cups sugar
¼ cup water
2 tablespoons rice wine vinegar
1½ teaspoons butter
1 teaspoon vanilla

In a medium saucepan over low heat, stir together the sugar, water, vinegar, and butter until sugar is dissolved. Turn heat up to medium and cook, without stirring, until the syrup reaches 265°F, as registered on a candy thermometer. Pour onto a buttered platter (be careful not to be splattered by the hot syrup—hold the pouring edge away from you and pour slowly) and let cool until a dent can be made in it when pressed with a finger. Sprinkle the vanilla on top and gather the taffy into a ball. Take care in picking up the mass; it could still be very hot in the center.

When you can touch it, start pulling it with your hands to a length of about 18 inches (see below). Then fold it back onto itself. Repeat

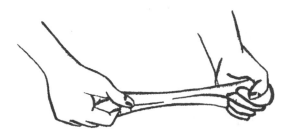

this action until the taffy becomes a crystal ribbon. Then start twisting as well as folding and pulling. (see above, left). Pull until the ridges begin to hold their shape.

Depending on your skill, the weather, and the cooking process, this can take between 5 and 20 minutes. Roll into long strips and cut into 1-inch pieces. Makes ½ pound.

201

Birthdays

Handmade Piñata

When I moved to California, I discovered that birthday parties for kids always included a piñata. Available at Mexican markets or party supply stores, they're great for kids under ten. But you can easily construct your own (and kids can help). Get a very large balloon and blow it up. Cut up newspaper into ½-inch strips. Dip each strip into a bowl of undiluted laundry starch. Then wrap the strip around the balloon. Continue until the balloon is completely covered. Allow to dry completely, then paint with poster paint and cut a hole in the top (the balloon will pop; that's okay) to drop the treats in it. On either side of the big hole, cut a small hole and insert a strong cord for the hanger. Fill the balloon with candy, small gifts, nuts, etc. (If you like, you can turn your piñata into a bird by adding construction paper head and wings, and crepe-paper feathers.) Suspend with a rope and pulley so you can raise and lower it while blindfolded adults and children take turns whacking it with a stick. When someone breaks it open, everyone scrambles for the goodies.

Easy Ideas for Kids' Birthday Parties

- Don't invite too many kids—one for each year of your child's life plus one is a good guideline.

- Keep the time short—ninety minutes is plenty, until the kids are older.

- Do a no-work-for-parents scavenger hunt. Make a list of things in nature—rocks, a maple leaf, acorns, ladybugs (be sure to set the insects free later)—that each team has to find.

- Host a movie day birthday party. Rent a couple of videos, make plenty of popcorn, and offer a variety of drinks and candy treats. Simple and fun for kids of all ages.

- How about a cookie party? Pick an easy recipe, and let the kids make the cookies, decorate, eat, or take them home. They can open presents while the cookies are baking.

- If your child's birthday isn't in the dead of winter, you can always go to a park and have a kite-flying party. Provide inexpensive kites (or make them) for each guest and a simple lunch, and let them run around as much as they want.

- Think about your child's interests and plan a theme party around that. He loves dinosaurs? Take him and four friends to the new dinosaur exhibit at the natural history museum. She loves to make things with her hands? Many cities have programs at community centers for kids to create an art project; some, for a fee, will even put on a party.

- Have a sneaker party. Have everyone bring a pair of clean white sneakers. Provide fabric markers, glitter, sequins, and let the kids go wild. Buy some fun wild laces for each child to add to the shoes.

203

Birthdays

Personalized Cookbooks

I try to give something meaningful to those I love for their birthdays and recently hit on a great idea. It all started when I began to paste recipes I clipped from magazines and newspapers in a blank book. Soon I had almost filled two books, and friends were asking me for a copy of this or that. One asked me for so many recipes I decided to make her a cookbook for her fiftieth birthday.

I bought a beautiful blank book, and divided it into sections with little tabs—appetizers, soups and salads, entrees, side dishes, and desserts. (I had learned the hard way that if you just place recipes randomly on pages, it's very hard to remember where your favorite mincemeat cookie recipe is: now it's somewhere in the beginning on the bottom of a left hand page. . . .) I then made chapter headings for each section, photocopied all the recipes she'd asked for, or had liked at my house, or I thought she'd liked, and gave it to her last year. She was thrilled.

That was the end of that—or so I thought. But when my college-aged daughter started complaining that she wanted a cookbook of easy gourmet dishes for college students, I knew I had to spring into action again. So that's what I'm working on now. I hope she gets as much pleasure out of receiving it as I have trying to figure out what to include.

Macadamias for Mom

We had been at the house of a relative who had a macadamia nut tree. My brother and I had collected a huge pile of nuts and brought them home with us, thinking they would be a birthday gift for our mother. When the day came, we woke up early, went to the back porch, and painfully (they are hard to crack) hammered them open for our mom. We then placed them into a large bowl, found a shell that had miraculously cracked perfectly in half, wrote a love note to our mom, and, folding it over and over, fit it into the shell and placed the shell on top of the nuts. I don't think she could have possibly slept through the racket, although she pretended to be surprised.

205

Birthdays

Saying It with Flowers

My husband is the most romantic person. The best birthday present I have gotten (so far) from him was a cardboard box he'd made and decorated with handmade paper and a dried flower. Inside the box were twelve blank cards, each with a different color photo of flowers that he had taken and pasted on the outside. The idea was that once a month, for an entire year, I could present him with one of the cards and he would buy me a bouquet of flowers and write me a love letter on the card. I felt so loved; I still have the box and all the love notes.

The Love Note Jar

This birthday, why not give your sweetheart a jar of love notes for his or her office? Simply buy an attractive jar, put a beautiful ribbon around it, and fill it with notes from your heart—"I love you because you are so gentle and kind," "I am so grateful that you are in my life"—whatever is true for you. Your honey can open them when he's having a bad day or feeling unappreciated and be reminded of your love.

The Day of Amber Light

My best birthday celebration was the one I spent all alone in a new city. It was my first year, first month, and first week away from home; I was off at college, thousands of miles away from my family and the world I knew. Not wanting to encumber my new college friends, I had told no one of the day's significance for me. I got up early and slipped out before my roommate woke up, and spent the entire day exploring the strange and utterly foreign place that I now found myself in. I walked up and down countless streets, finding myself pleasantly lost and, strangely, completely unafraid. Every cobbled courtyard, burbling fountain, and charming medieval building seemed especially shined and settled for my enjoyment. I was particularly delighted, rounding the corner on a deserted and sun-struck alley late in the afternoon, to happen upon a ponderous gentleman, seated on an old stone bench, which upon closer inspection I realized was hewn of old and weathered bronze. I fell in love with that softly worn, old-fashioned city that day, and though I continue to visit it often, that day of golden amber autumn light will always be my special, private treasure.

207

Birthdays

Beading Together

One great way to entertain kids at a birthday party is to buy an assortment of inexpensive beads (bead and craft stores abound these days) and host a beading party. If you have very young children, you can use dry macaroni (instead of beads that can be popped into mouths) that they can decorate with paint or glitter. You can then help kids string them onto elastic for easy bracelets and necklaces. For older beaders, buy bead thread, beading needles, and clasps to finish off their creations.

Kitchen Clay

You can also have kids make their own beads or medallions out of flour clay. (This works well for Christmas ornaments too; simply use cookie cutters to create the shapes and poke a hole at the top with a darning needle before cooking.) Mix 4 cups of white flour, 1 cup salt, and 1½ cups water together until well blended. Knead for five minutes, then roll out and mold to desired shape. Slide the beads onto nails so they can be strung later. Bake for 30 minutes in a 350°F oven, or until beads are hardened, but not brown or they will get brittle. Cool completely with nails still on. When cool, remove nails, paint with acrylics, glaze with clear enamel and put on nylon fishline, leather thongs, or dental floss.

With the One I Love

My favorite birthdays are planned events. Since my partner and I love to travel and since our birthdays are in May, we try to celebrate by being together in a specially designated birthday location. For my fortieth, we climbed the Mayan temples of Tikal in Guatemala. This year we took the scenic "Philosophers' Walk" in Kyoto, Japan. One year we ate at a famous brasserie in Paris. The location is not always so exotic—the most important part is to share a unique experience with my best friend. Then I am always happy on my birthday.

209

Birthdays

Dinner Out

The birthday tradition in our family was that on your birthday we got to go out alone with our parents to a fancy restaurant of our choice, leaving the other kids home with the babysitter. It was a special time, a chance to wear your best dress and to have all the adult attention lavished on you. Since my birthday is right before Christmas, I always chose a restaurant in an old inn that had beautiful decorations in every room. First, I would order drinks—I had the Shirley

Temple—then I would have a wonderful steak, some fabulous dessert, look at all the ornaments and lights, and go home fabulously satisfied.

Handmade Trivets

Here's a great birthday gift. Get a plain white or terra-cotta tile at a craft store. Draw a design on it with a china-graph pencil (available at craft stores)—little kids can do handprints, which are always relished by doting parents. Then paint in your design using model paints. When completely dry, coat it with plain ceramic varnish.

Chocolate Delight

I've always been a chocolate connoisseur. This highlight of the birthday parties of my childhood gives you the ticket to indulge yourself—after some work. After a hectic struggle with dice, woolens, and utensils, the piece of chocolate that actually lands in your mouth and slowly melts on your tongue is a true pleasure.

You'll need a hat, mittens, shawl, knife and fork, one bar of chocolate, 2 dice, and four to eight participants. The participants sit around a small table with the wrapped bar of chocolate, knife and fork, hat, mittens, shawl and dice placed in the middle of the table. Each participant rolls the dice once to determine who starts the game. Start rolling the dice as you pass them around the table, until one participant rolls a pair. The person who rolled the pair immediately puts on the hat, wraps the shawl around his neck, slips on the mittens, and, after unwrapping the chocolate, uses the knife and fork to eat as much of the chocolate as possible. All the while, the other participants continue rolling the dice until another person rolls a pair. This is the signal for the chocolate-eating participant to drop the knife and fork and quickly pass the hat, shawl, and mittens to the person with the lucky strike. Never touch the chocolate without the knife and fork, and don't start to cut before the hat, shawl, and mittens are in their proper place. Continue the game until there's no chocolate left.

Birthdays

Easy Chocolate Soufflé

I don't like cake and so it was a tradition in my family to have a chocolate soufflé on my birthday. But it's not the easiest thing in the world to do. However, recently I found this fabulous fun and delicious recipe that—believe it or not—can be made in advance! Just prepare all ingredients the night before and refrigerate, then pop into the oven 20 minutes prior to serving.

¼ cup unsalted butter
5 squares semisweet chocolate, chopped
3 eggs, separated
½ cup sugar
½ cup flour
2 tablespoons cocoa powder
½ teaspoons vanilla
whipped cream or raspberry sauce, optional

Preheat oven to 375°F. Heat butter and chocolate together until completely melted (you can do this in the microwave for about 2 minutes). Stir until smoothly blended. In a separate bowl, beat egg whites at medium speed until foamy, then gradually beat in sugar. Continue beating until stiff peaks form. Add yolks, flour, cocoa powder, and vanilla to the chocolate mixture. Gently fold in approximately ⅓ of the egg white mixture, then gradually add the remainder. Spoon into four 6-ounce ramekins or baking dish, and bake 15 to 20 minutes on a jelly roll pan until tops are puffed. Top with whipped cream or raspberry sauce, if desired. Serves 4.

Edible Tribute

My teenaged uncle baby-sat us on many weekends when I was growing up, usually sleeping over on Saturday night and having breakfast with us on Sunday. One such Sunday happened to be my mother's birthday, and we cooked up a plan of waking up early to make breakfast for her. The main course was to be pancakes, lovingly shaped to spell "MOM." (I think he got the idea from a Boy Scout cookbook or something....) We stood over the stove for what seemed like an eternity, trying to pour out two perfect M's and just one O, but they all broke when we tried to flip them. I was happy to stuff myself on the huge pile of mistakes, while my brother was determined to get three intact letters. Tension built as the batter supply decreased and the likelihood Mom would wake up increased. With the last ladle of batter, we did successfully complete the edible tribute. And yes, she was surprised!

213

Birthdays

Love Cards

My husband-to-be started a birthday tradition the first year we met (although I'm sure at the time he had no idea he was starting a tradition.) For the past three years he has been making my birthday cards. He's very creative by nature (he's a senior art director at an advertising agency), so the cards come naturally to him. I treasure his cards and have plans on putting together a scrapbook to memorialize them.

214

A Basket of Love

I love to make birthday baskets—and they are so easy. Simply find a pretty basket, spray paint it any color you like (sand paper it slightly first so the paint will stick better), add a pretty ribbon to the handle, and fill it with the birthday person's favorite things: chocolate-covered cherries, sexy underwear, skin lotion, whatever he or she fancies.

Scented Notepaper

You can make a wonderful birthday present for a loved one that will add a personal touch to his or her correspondence: scented stationery. It's incredibly simple. This makes enough for you and your loved ones.

8 ounces unscented talcum powder
15 drops of your favorite essential oil
or perfume
6 small, closely woven cotton or
silk bags, open on one side
ribbon
notepaper and envelopes
1 plastic bag

In a bowl, combine the powder and perfume. Cover tightly and let sit for a day. Spoon the mixture into the bags and tie with ribbon. Place the bags in between the layers of notepaper and envelopes in a box and put the box into the plastic bag. Allow to sit for a few days so that the scent will permeate the paper. Makes 6 sachets.

Birthdays

Cone Cakes

Here's a fun way to serve cake at your child's next birthday party. You can be sure that the kids will be clamoring for more than one.

24 flat-bottomed ice cream cones
1 package (17–24 ounces) cake mix
muffin tins
frosting and cake decorations of your choice

Prepare the cake mix according to package directions. Spoon the batter into the cones until they are ⅔ full. Place the cones in the muffin tins and bake according to package directions for cupcakes. When cones are cool, frost and decorate. Makes 24.

Easy Ideas for Meaningful Birthdays

Rather than spending money on elaborate parties or expensive gifts, why not allow the occasion of a birthday to focus attention and love on the birthday person? Here are some suggestions to get you started:

- Tell the story of your child's birth (or some other memorable event in which he is the star) every year on his birthday.

- Ask the birthday celebrant to talk about the most memorable event of her past year. Ask her to talk about what she is most looking forward to now that she is ten (or fifty or...)

- Go around the table and ask everyone to say one thing they really love about the birthday person, or have each person in the family write a short note in advance and place them in a nice notebook. You can add to it every year.

- Let the birthday person choose the menu or cook something you know he loves and you don't have often. My stepson adores my tomatoes with goat cheese dressing, so I am sure to serve it every year for him. It doesn't have to be dinner—what about a birthday breakfast?

- A great one for kids: Start a memory chest for each of your children. Put in Great Aunt Tilly's famous latke recipe, Grandma's silver tea service, a drawing he did when he was three. Each birthday, add one item to the box. Let her look inside and tell her that someday all these treasures will be hers (anticipation breeds excitement!). Present it to her when she leaves home.

- Keep a journal of your thoughts about him that you record each year on his birthday. After several years, give it to him.

- Make something special with your own hands: a chair, a stuffed animal, a quilt. My father and grandfather made me a dollhouse for my birthday when I was four, which I loved and have now given to my daughter on her fourth birthday.

Birthdays

- Create a photo album just for the birthday person. After dinner, gather around and go through the pictures and let everyone reminisce.

- Instead of a mass-produced card, try making one of your own. Remember those paper-doily cards you made as a kid? Chances are, your birthday person would love one, particularly if you write specifically about why you love him or her. The words don't have to be fancy, just from your heart.

- If you live far away from family or friends, send letters each year on their birthday telling them why you love them. It can be as simple as: "I love you because . . . you bake me my favorite cookies," "you always keep in touch," "you always tell me the truth."

A Homey Bed and Breakfast

I had been going through a rough time—I had just ended a fourteen-year relationship, was living in a tiny studio apartment, and my fortieth birthday was coming up. My dear friend Molly suggested that I come to her house for a real pampering weekend in honor of my birthday. When I arrived she had prepared the guest room with fresh flowers and fruit, a stack of magazines, and a nest of pillows. The guest bathroom had a inflatable pillow, an array of bath oils, and a candle. I lay around reading, soaked in her tub (I had only a shower), and sat quietly by the fire with her after a delicious dinner. I cried a lot, talked a little, and generally felt very taken care of. It was one of my best birthdays ever.

Finger Paint

Here's a kids' party idea—first the kids make the paint, then they create their own paintings to take home with them.

1½ cups liquid laundry starch
1½ cups laundry powder
mixing bowl
tempera paint

small plastic containers with lids
plastic spoons

Mix together the laundry starch and the laundry powder. Stir until smooth. Pour equal parts of the mixture into bowls and add a different color of paint to each bowl. Stir with a spoon until the color is well-mixed. This paint will run while wet, so give it time to dry on a level surface.

219

Birthdays

Easy Ideas for *Your* Birthday

It's easy to dread birthdays as we get older. Somehow they don't have the sparkle they did when we were little. Here are some ways to make them shine:

- Don't be afraid to ask for what you *really* want. There's nothing more pleasurable than getting your heart's desire. Loved ones aren't mind-readers—if you want a white kitten, say so, or you might end up with a python.

- Take time to reflect on your life—where are you, what matters to you now? What is pulling you into your future? Perhaps you might want to write down your commitments to yourself for the next year and post them somewhere handy.

- Do something you've always wanted to do but have never dared: a big thing like a trip to the Yucatan, or a small thing like riding on a friend's motorcycle.

- Give yourself away—volunteer for the day at a soup kitchen or give a donation to your favorite charity (a dollar for every year, perhaps?).

220

The Mass Birthday Party

I come from a big extended family whose members all live in Northern California. As we were growing up, it got to be too much to have birthday parties for all the aunts, uncles, grandparents, and cousins. Plus there were a whole bunch of us born within a month or so of one another. So my grandparents had the idea for us all to go away together each summer to a resort and to have a mass birthday party during the week. One year when I was about six, the aunts were bringing in the presents to be handed out later in the week. All the gifts were wrapped except one—a big black stuffed dog. All the cousins—aged two to eight—hoped that dog was for them. We spent all week talking about it and trying to get our aunt to tell us who was the lucky recipient. The day came and the dog was the last present. And it was for me!

All You Can Eat

My dad and I always celebrated ice cream birthdays. We would walk to the corner Baskin Robbins and each order a single cone, any flavor we wanted. We would then walk around, eating, until we were finished. Then we would return to the store and repeat the process until both of us were completely satisfied. (I think when I turned fourteen, my record was six cones—all strawberry.) My father has been gone for decades now, but the smell of ice cream still brings those birthdays back to me.

221

Birthdays

Do Nothing Birthday

I was one of those '80s-generation kids whose time was completely structured. Because my single mom worked full-time, I had to be either in school or in some after-school activity; ditto for the summers. The weekends were filled with things that couldn't get done during the week—chores, shopping, sports. I longed to have time in which to do absolutely nothing—I used to beg my mother to be able to stay home for at least one day when I wasn't sick. Then she got the idea for Do Nothing Birthdays. Every year on my birthday, I would stay home from school and she would take off from work. The night before, I would stay up as late as I wanted, then I would sleep as long as I wanted in the morning, and eat exactly what I pleased throughout the day. Mom would be at my beck and call; whatever I decided I wanted to do, she would go along with—an afternoon movie, a pony ride, whatever. The following weekend, I would have some kind of party with other kids, but it's those Do Nothing Days that I really cherished.

The Way to a Man's Heart

I live alone and I hate to cook, but I do love to eat. One year for my birthday, my mother sent me via overnight mail, packed in ice, a month's worth of homemade frozen meals. All my favorite dishes—spaghetti with meatballs, chicken enchiladas, chili. That was a present I'll never forget.

Meals on Wheels

Creating such a birthday gift is easy—provided you have plenty of Tupperware and freezer space. Simply double your main course recipes for a few weeks and freeze the leftovers in plastic containers. When you have enough, deliver your gift. If you don't live within driving distance, this will require a bit more work and money—a plastic-lined box filled with ice (dry ice would be even better), and an overnight delivery service.

Red Velvet Cake

Every year for my birthday my mother would make Red Velvet Cake with chocolate frosting for me. It has become such an important part of my birthday tradition that even now that I am in my forties, someone, usually my husband, makes it for me. The few times I didn't have it, I felt bereft. I hope it brings you a bit of the pleasure it has brought for me.

Birthdays

½ cup butter, margarine, or shortening
1½ cups sugar
2 eggs
1 teaspoon vanilla
3 tablespoons cocoa
2 ounces red food coloring
2½ cups sifted cake flour
1 cup buttermilk
1 teaspoon salt
1 teaspoon baking soda
1 tablespoon white vinegar

Preheat oven to 350° F. Cream shortening and sugar until smooth. Add eggs and vanilla. Beat well. In a separate bowl, blend cocoa and food coloring; add to sugar mixture. Add flour, buttermilk, and salt alternatively. Mix soda and vinegar in cup and add to batter.

Bake in two greased and floured 9-inch cake pans for 30 to 35 minutes or until a toothpick inserted in the center comes out clean. Let cool before frosting.

Lei Day

I come from Hawaii and we always give a lei on an important occasion—weddings, birthdays, graduations, homecomings, housewarmings. I always love to make them for all my friends on their birthdays. Sometimes I choose the flower of the Hawaiian *alii* (royalty), the beautiful and delicate *ilima*, millions of petals of which are required to string a single lei; other times the richly fragrant leaves of the *maile* vine, the wearing of which traditionally symbolizes victory. The sultry scent of the fragile *pikake* (Tahitian ginger) and the sweet, honeyed aroma of the common *plumeria* (fragipani) combine with the fragrances of countless other flowers, creating a sultry perfume that is the essence of Hawaii.

Homemade Leis

Leis can be easily strung using a variety of flowers. Some of the best are: tuberoses, roses (use buds, not open flowers), carnations, and asters. You will need a long (1 to 2 inches) sewing needle, and unscented dental floss, and at least three dozen blossoms of any of the above flowers. Measure a length of the floss around your neck; leis are most comfortable when they reach nearly to your natural waist. String a bead or make a large knot in one end of the floss. Trim each flower so that only the blossom remains; then, starting from the stem end, insert the needle and push through the center of the blossom, and out the other end. (You may be more comfortable wearing a thimble.) Continue until the string is full, with ¼ inch remaining to be tied off (you will probably need more flowers than you think!). Leis can also be made with paper flowers or candy; even dry cereal! They make excellent centerpieces, too.

225

Birthdays

Enduring Love

When I was little, my mom and I used to argue about who loved the other more. So last year, when I found the following card, I had to send it to her for her birthday. It read:

"Mom, I love you more than you love me, because you have only loved me for part of your life, and I have loved you all of mine." She loved it.

Her First Step

My forty-year-old daughter found an old snapshot of me holding her hand as she took her first step. She had it blown up, hand tinted, and framed for me for my birthday last year. Boy, did it bring back memories—it's my favorite possession.

Surprise Breakfast

One of the best birthdays I had was when my four-year-old Jed (with Mom's help) arranged a surprise breakfast for me. I am usually the one who is in charge of making breakfast, but on this morning I was allowed to sleep late. When I woke up to his little smiling face hovering over the bed, Jed told me to come to the table. There I found a note saying that my breakfast was hidden somewhere in the back yard. Off I went on a treasure hunt that finally led me to a box containing a bowl of cereal and a banana. Jed laughed his head off with delight watching me try to find where he hid it. Then we all sat down on the grass, coffee magically appeared, and we ate. What fun!

Birthdays

Cracking Up

I was born on Christmas (and my mother and father also have birthdays that week as well). So every year since I can remember, I have celebrated on my half-birthday. As an adult, I always hold a birthday barbecue bash on my deck for all my friends. I serve sangria to the adults and lemonade to the kids, ask everyone to bring their own food to barbecue, make a big vat of potato salad, and *voilà!* We feast and laugh, and all of us—kids and grownups—play silly birthday games like Red Rover and Blind Man's Bluff, and we have a grand old time. One year, I read about an activity that has since become a standard. It's a bit messy, but guaranteed to turn any ordinary party into a revelry: Confetti Eggs. I make a few dozen in advance and when the time is right, we all run around cracking them over each other's heads. You can imagine the results.

Confetti Eggs

raw eggs
fingernail scissors
confetti

Do this over a large bowl. With the fingernail scissors, cut a small hole at one end of the egg and a larger hole, about the size of a nickel, at the other. Clean out the egg by blowing into the small hole and allowing the insides to come out the large hole into the bowl. (Use the eggs in cooking.) Rinse each shell carefully with water and allow to dry. Fill the egg with confetti through the large hole, then tape up the holes until ready to use. Crack each over an unsuspecting person.

Angelic Rememberance

Ever since I can remember, my mother made me angel food cake with pink peppermint boiled frosting for my birthday. I always loved it, but my poor sister, whose birthday followed mine by six weeks, did not, and my mother would often forget and make it for her too. (Which only goes to show that simple pleasures are idiosyncratic.) I loved that cake so much and have made such a fuss about it as an adult that the men in my life learned that a birthday wasn't complete unless it was accompanied by an angel food cake. (And believe me, although I never complained, I can really taste the difference between store-bought, made from a package, and homemade.) So here's the real thing. Feel free to frost it any way you want, but for my money, nothing beats the boiled frosting recipe in the old *Joy of Cooking*.

Angel Food Cake

1¼ cups cake flour
½ cup sugar
12 egg whites at room temperature
¼ teaspoon salt
1¼ teaspoons cream of tartar
1 teaspoon vanilla
¼ teaspoon almond extract
1⅓ cups sugar

229

Birthdays

Preheat oven to 375°F. Sift flour with ½ cup sugar four times. Combine egg whites, salt, cream of tartar, vanilla, and almond extract in large bowl. Beat with a flat wire whip, rotary beater, or high speed of electric mixer until moist, glossy, soft peaks form. Add 1⅓ cups sugar, sprinkling in ⅓ cup at a time and beating until blended after each addition, about 25 strokes by hand. Sift in flour mixture in four additions, folding in by hand after each addition and turning bowl often. After last addition, use 10 to 20 extra strokes. Pour into ungreased 10-inch tube pan. Bake for 35 to 40 minutes, or until the top springs back when pressed lightly. Invert on rack and cool thoroughly. Then remove from pan. Serve with frosting of your choice. Serves 8.

The Phone Call

For fourteen years, I was the stepmother of Michael, whom I helped raise from the age of two. Childless myself, I had the usual kinds of stepmother difficulties—the sense of second-class citizenship, the lack of social structures supporting my role, a sense of competitiveness from his mother, even my name (for all those years, even when he lived with us full-time, he always called me by my first name). Then, abruptly, his father and I broke up at the beginning of the year. I moved out. I was sure that would be the end of that with Michael. We were never particularly close, and what does a teenager do with an ex-stepmother anyway? So when the phone rang at 9:30 P.M. the evening of my birthday, I was shocked to hear sixteen-year-old Michael's voice: "Just calling to wish you a Happy Birthday," he said, "and to thank you for all you did for me over the years." Nothing has pleased me more than that phone call.

Index

A

A Day in the Life album, 59
Adult Sleepover, 156
All You Can Eat, 221
Angel Food Cake, 229
Angel, gilded, 112
Aplets, 7
Apricot Rugelach, 67
Aromatic Indulgences, 175

B

Basket of Love, 214
Bath Salts, *see* Spicy Bath Salts
Beading Together, 207–08
Bird Feeder, *see* Pine Cone Bird Feeder
Birthdays, *see* Kids' and Adults'
    Birthdays
Blending Traditions, 88–89
Board Games, 158
Bonfire Night, *see* Guy Fawkes Day
Bow Sachets, 100
Box of Memories, 104
Boxing Day, 137-142
Braised Ginger Pork, 181
Breads
    Garlic Bread, 141
    Homemade Flour Tortillas, 22
    Pumpkin Bread, 33
    Soda Bread, 170
Breakfast
    Edible Tribute, 213
    Matzo Brie, 71
Surprise Breakfast, 226–27
Broccoli Salad, 50
Bubble Bath, *see* Homemade Bubble
    Bath

C

Cakes
    Angel Food Cake, 229
    Cone Cakes, 215
    Red Velvet Cake, 223
Candied Sweet Potatoes, 40
Candles
    homemade, 26, 108
    Kanara, homemade, 150
    Personally Scented Candles, 108
    symbolism, 62
Candy Cane Cookies, 126
Candy Cane Potpourri, 105
Carmel Corn, 7
Caroling on Christmas, 89, 90
Catalogs
    Aroma Therapeutix, 175
    Back to Basics Toys, 121
    Bare Escentuals catalog and stores,
        175
    The Body Shop catalog and stores,
        175
    Body Time catalog and stores, 175
    Earthsake stores, 175
    Gooseberry Patch, 124
    Green World Mercantile, 175
    Harmony Catalog, 122

Catalogs *continued*
  Hearthsong, 26, 175
  Indiana Botanic Gardens, 102
  Lavender Lane, 102
  Red Rose catalog and stores, 175
  Rosemary House, 102
Celebration for Two, 162
Cheese Soufflé, 163
Children (*see also* Crafts, Games)
  Beading Together, 207–08
  Dinner Out, 209–10
  Family Time, 160–61
  Finger Paint, 218–19
  Kitchen Clay, 208
Chinese Almond Cookies, 184
Chinese New Year, 179-187
  parade, 182-184
Chocolate Delight, 210
Christmas, 95-135
  decorations, 96, 102, 111, 112,
    113–14, 122-23
  ornaments, 103, 104
  pledge, 96
  spirit, 99–100
  stockings, 104, 105
  tree, 97–99, 118–19
Christmas Eve, 85-93
Christmas Eve Gift, 86
Clam Chowder, 140
Classic Caramels, 8
Cone Cakes, 215
Confetti Eggs, 228
Cookie Cutters, 124
Cookie Making, 128
Cookies
  Candy Cane Cookies, 126
  Chinese Almond Cookies, 184
  Gingerbread, 123

Greek Kourabiedes, 127
Handprint Cookies, 124
Mexican Wedding Cookies, 23
Mincemeat Cookies, 43
Snowball Surprises, 125
Crafts (*see also* Decorations, Gifts)
  Dried Rose Heart, 148
  Family History Book, 145
  Gilded Angel, 112
  Homemade Candles, 26
  Homemade Paper, 61
  Kindness Box, 91
  Kitchen Clay, 208
  Papier-Mâché Flower Vase, 96
  Pine Cone Bird Feeder, 64
  Scented Notepaper, 214
Cranberry Apple Waldorf, 41
Cranberry Punch, 52
Creating Connection, 46
Creating Family Unity, 146–47
Crème Brûlée, see *Quick Crème
  Brûlée*

D
Decorations
  Christmas, 112, 113–14, 118
  Fragrant Candles, 108
  Halloween, 2-3
  Holiday Napkin Rings, 65
  Hydrangea Wreath, 122
  Kanara, 150
  Mistletoe Ball, 111
  Papier-Mâché Flower Vase, 96
  Personally Scented Candles, 108
  Scented Ornaments, 103
  Thanksgiving, 41, 50
  Winter Solstice, 77–78
Decorative Choker, 117

Desserts (*see also* Cakes, Cookies)
    Aplets, 7
    Apricot Rugelach, 67
    Caramel Corn, 7
    Classic Caramels, 8
    Cranberry Apple Waldorf, 41
    Easy Chocolate Soufflé, 211
    Easy Stollen, 132
    Gulab Jamun, 192
    Old-Fashioned Plum Pudding, 120
    Old-Fashioned Rice Pudding, 77
    Peanut Brittle, 9
    Persimmon Pudding, 53
    Quick Crème Brûlée, 164
    Red Velvet Cake, 223
    Ten-Minute Fudge, 38
    Vanilla Taffy, 200
Dinner Out, 209–10
Doing Nothing, 170, 221–22
Dreidel, 56-57, 62-64
Dried Fruit Stuffing, 37
Dried Rose Heart, 148
Drinks
    Cranberry Punch, 52
    Eighteen-Carat Eggnog, 156
    Hot Buttered Rum, 90
    Mexican Hot Chocolate, 23
    Nature's Hangover Cure, 172
    Wassail, 81

E
Easy Ideas for …
    Caroling, 90
    Celebrating Chinese New Year,
        186–87
    Celebrating Yule, 82
    Cookie Making, 128
    Creating Connection, 46

    Halloween Parties, 5–6
    Inexpensive Decorations, 113–14
    Kids' Birthday Parties, 202–03
    Making Christmas Manageable,
        108–09
    Making Hanukkah Special, 66–67
    Making New Year's Day
        Meaningful, 171–72
    Meaninfgul Birthdays, 216–17
    Pleasurable Holidays, xvii–xviii
    Simple Costumes, 12–13
    Thanksgiving Decorations, 50–51
    Your Birthday, 219–20
Easy Chocolate Soufflé, 211
Easy Stollen, 132
Edible Tribute, 213
Eighteen-Carat Eggnog, 156
Entrees
    Braised Ginger Pork, 181
    Cheese Soufflé, 162
    Clam Chowder, 140
    Holiday Ham, 116
    Hoppin' John, 173
    Kibbeh Onion and Tomato Stew, 194
    Lamb Stew, 4
    Pepper-Coated Lamb, 44
    Seafood Gumbo, 151
    Tamale Pie, 21

F
Family History Book, 145
Family Time, 160–61
Festival of Lights, *see* Hanukkah
Finger Paint, 218
Flowers
    Leis, 224, 225
    Flower Barrettes, 118
    Hydrangea Wreath, 122

Flowers *continued*
    Papier-Mâché Flower Vase, 96
    Saying it With Flowers, 205–06
Football Fun, 176
Fortune Cookies, 158
Fragrances
    Aromatic Indulgences, 175
    Bow Sachets, 100
    Candy Cane Potpourri, 105
    Frayed Nerves Bath, 175
    Homemade Bubble Bath, 60
    Lavender Bath Powder, 129
    New Year's Potpourri, 177
    Personally Scented Candles, 108
    Rose Potpourri, 101
    Scented Notepaper, 214
    Scented Ornaments, 103
    Yule Log, 83

G
Games
    Board Games , 158
    Chocolate Delight, 210–11
    Confetti Eggs, 228
    Dreidel, 56-57, 62-64
    Football Fun, 176
    Handmade Piñata, 201–02
Garlic Bread, 141
Gastronomic Travel, 159
Ghoul-Aid, 6
Gift of Love, 110
Gifts (*see also* Crafts)
    A Basket of Love, 214
    Bow Sachets, 100
    A Day in the Life album, 59
    Decorative Choker, 117
    Edible Tribute, 213
    Family History Book, 145

Flower Barrettes, 118
Fortune Cookies, 158
Gift of Love, 110
Handmade Trivets, 210
Hand-tinted snapshot, 226
Herbal Soap Balls, 154
Homemade Bubble Bath, 60
A Homey Bed and Breakfast, 218
A Jar of Good Fortune, 158
Lavender Bath Powder, 129
Love Note Jar, 206
Macadamias for Mom, 205
Magic Reindeer Food, 91
Meals on Wheels, 222–23
Nonmaterial Gifts, 147
One at a Time, 129
Papier-Mâché Flower Vase, 96
Personalized Cookbooks, 204
Picasso Pillow, 109
Rose Potpourri, 101
Saying it with Flowers, 205–06
Scented Notepaper, 214
Seven Nights of Gifts, 72
Surprise Breakfast, 226–27
Gilded Angel, 112
Gingerbread, 123
Giving
    Creating Connection, 46
    Giving Back, 13
    Giving Yourself, 51
    Random Acts of Holiday
        Kindness, 121–22
    The Spirit of Giving, 133–34
Great Greens, 153
Greek Kourabiedes, 127
Guest of Honor, 87
Gulab Jamun, 192
Guy Fawkes Day, 29-34

H

Halloween, 1-15
    costumes, 6, 11–13
    decorations, 2-3
    parties, 5
Handmade Piñata, 201–02
Handmade Trivets, 210
Handprint Cookies, 124
Hand-tinted snapshot, 226
Hangover Cure, see *Nature's
    Hangover Cure*
Hanukkah, 55-72
    Festival of Lights, 62
    Seven Nights of Gifts, 72
Hard Sauce, 121
Herbal Soap Balls, 154
Hogmanay, 165–67
Holiday Ham, 116
Holiday Ideas
    Adult Sleepover, 156
    All You Can Eat, 221
    Blending Traditions, 88–89
    A Box of Memories, 104
    Celebration for Two, 162
    Christmas Eve Gift, 86
    Creating Family Unity, 146–47
    The Day Doesn't Matter, 130
    Doing Nothing, 170, 221–22
    Gastronomic Travel, 159
    Guest of Honor, 87
    The North Pole Christmas
        Mission Website, 99–100
    One at a Time, 129
    Open House, 177–78
Holiday Napkin Rings, 65–66
Holiday Spirit
    Kindness Box, 91
    Love Pledges, 161–62

    The Spirit of Giving, 133–34
    The True Christmas Spirit, 99–100
Homemade Bubble Bath, 60
Homemade Candles, 26
Homemade Flour Tortillas, 22
Homemade *Kanara*, 150
Homemade Paper, 61
Homey Bed and Breakfast, 218
Hoppin' John, 173
Hot Buttered Rum, 90
Hydrangea Wreath, 122

I

'Id al-Fitr, 189-195

J

Jar of Good Fortune, 158

K

Kanara, homemade, 150
Karamu Feast, 150-154
Kibbeh Onion and Tomato Stew, 194
Kids' and Adults Birthdays, 197–230
Kindness Box, 91
Kitchen Clay, 208
Kwanzaa, 143-154

L

Lamb Stew, 4
Latkes, see *Saul's Hanukkah Latkes*
Lavender Bath Powder, 129
Leis, 224, 225
Love Note Jar, 206
Love Pledges, 161–62

M

Macadamias for Mom, 205
Magic Reindeer Food, 91–92

Matzo Brie, 71
Meals on Wheels, 222–23
Meaningful Birthdays, 216
Mexican Day of the Dead, 17–27
Mexican Hot Chocolate, 23
Mexican Wedding Cookies, 23
Mincemeat Cookies, 42
Mistletoe Ball, 111

N
Napkin Rings, *see* Holiday Napkin
    Rings
Natural Stockings, 105
Nature's Hangover Cure, 172
New Year's Day, 169-178
New Year's Eve, 155-167
New Year's Potpourri, 177
New Year's Soak, 174
Nonmaterial Gifts, 147–48
North Pole Christmas Mission
    Website, 99–100

O
Old-Fashioned Plum Pudding, 120
Old-Fashioned Rice Pudding, 77
Old-Fashioned Toys, 121
One at a Time, 129
Onion Soup, 32

P
Papier-Mâché Flower Vase, 96
Parades
    Chinese New Years' Parade,
        182–84
    Tournament of Roses Parade,
        159–60
Peanut Brittle, 9

Peanut Butter Soup, 151
Pepper-Coated Lamb, 44
Persimmon Pudding, 53
Personalized Cookbooks, 204
Picasso Pillow, 109–10
Pine Cone Bird Feeder, 64
Pleasurable Holidays, xvii–xviii
Plum Pudding, see *Old-Fashioned Plum
    Pudding*
Potpourri, 101, 102, 105, 177
Pumpkin Bread, 33

Q
Quick Crème Brûlée, 164

R
Random Acts of Holiday Kindness,
    121–22
Red Velvet Cake, 223
Rose Potpourri, 101

S
Salads
    Broccoli Salad, 50
    Tomato Avocado Salad, 20
Saul's Hanukkah Latkes, 58
Saying it With Flowers, 205–06
Scented Notepaper, 214
Scented Ornaments, 103
Seafood Gumbo, 151
Seven Nights of Gifts, 72
Seven Principles of Kwanzaa, 149–50
Side Dishes and Snacks
    Dried Fruit Stuffing, 37
    Homemade Flour Tortillas, 22
    Saul's Hanukkah Latkes, 58
    Snack Peas, 60

Side Dishes and Snacks *continued*
   Spicy Cranberry Relish, 48
Snack Peas, 60
Snowball Surprises, 125
Soda Bread, 170
Soups
   Clam Chowder, 140
   Onion Soup, 32
   Peanut Butter Soup, 151
Spicy Bath Salts, 80
Spicy Cranberry Relish, 48
Spirit of Giving, 133–34
Stollen, see *Easy Stollen*
Surprise Breakfast, 226–27
Sweet Potato Pie, 153

T
Tamale Pie, 21
Ten-Minute Fudge, 38
Thanksgiving, 35-54
   centerpiece, 41
   decorations, 50
Tomato Avocado Salad, 20
Tournament of Roses Parade, *see*
   Parades

True Christmas Spirit, 99–100

V
Vanilla Taffy, 200
Vegetables
   Broccoli Salad, 50
   Candied Sweet Potatoes, 40
   Great Greens, 153
   Kibbeh Onion and Tomato Stew, 194

W
Wassail, 81
Winter Solstice, 73-84
   decorations, 77–78
Worm Dessert, 6
Wrapping paper, *see* Homemade
   Paper

Y
Your Birthday, 219–20
Yule, *see* Winter Solstice
Yule Log, 74, 83

OTHER *SIMPLE PLEASURES* BOOKS FROM CONARI PRESS

*Simple Pleasures: Soothing Suggestions and
Small Comforts for Living Well Year Round*

*Simple Pleasures of the Garden: Stories, Recipies,
and Crafts from the Abundant Earth*

*C*onari Press, established in 1987, publishes books on topics ranging from psychology, spirituality, and women's history to parenting and personal growth. Our main goal is to publish quality books that will make a difference in people's lives—both how we feel about ourselves and how we relate to one another.

Our readers are our most important resource, and we value your input, suggestions, and ideas. We'd love to hear from you—after all, we are publishing books for you!

To request our latest book catalog, or to be added to our mailing list, please contact:

CONARI PRESS

2550 Ninth Street, Suite 101
Berkeley, California 94710-2551
800-685-9595 • fax: 510-649-7190
e-mail: conari@conari.com
www.conari.com